PIRATE QUEEN

For Daisy

PIRATE QUEEN

The Life of
Grace O'Malley
1530–1603

JUDITH COOK

MERCIER PRESS

Mercier Press
Douglas Village, Cork
www.mercierpress.ie

Trade enquiries to CMD Distribution
55A Spruce Avenue, Stillorgan Industrial Park,
Blackrock, Co. Dublin
Email: cmd@columbia.ie

ISBN 1 85635 443 1

10 9 8 7 6 5 4 3 2 1

A CIP record for this title is available from the British Library

Typeset by Palimpsest Book Production Limited,
Polmont, Stirlingshire
Printed in Great Britain by Creative Print and Design,
Ebbw Vale, Wales

Contents

Illustrations

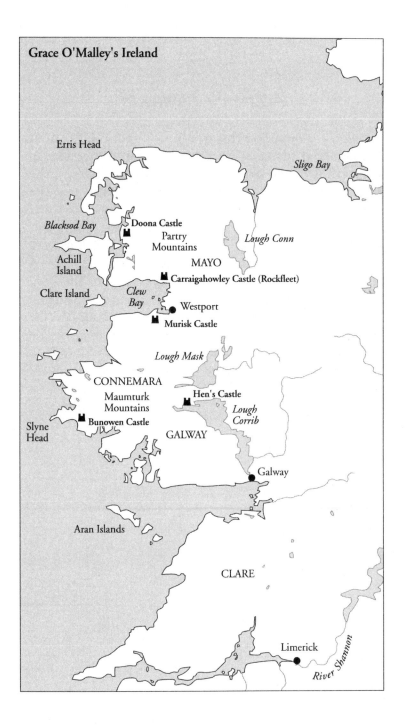

Grace O'Malley's Ireland

Erris Head

Sligo Bay

Blacksod Bay

Doona Castle

Partry
Mountains

Lough Conn

Achill
Island

MAYO

Carraigahowley Castle (Rockfleet)

Clare Island

Clew
Bay

Westport

Murisk Castle

Lough Mask

CONNEMARA

Maumturk
Mountains

Hen's Castle

Lough
Corrib

Slyne
Head

Bunowen Castle

GALWAY

Galway

Aran Islands

CLARE

Limerick

River Shannon

Acknowledgements

As ever, a project like this would be impossible without the help and advice of libraries. My thanks therefore to the staff of the Bodleian Library, the British Library, the Public Record Office, Trinity College, Dublin and the Morrab Library in Penzance which now has its own Celtic Studies section. The various librarians were not only sympathetic when I used their facilities but were extremely helpful in answering my e-mails and making suggestions as to what was available. Also to the very useful bibliography of State Papers (Domestic) and the State Papers of Ireland researched by Anne Chambers for her own book, *Granuaille*, and for the assistance of the Galway Tourist Board. Last but not least, my thanks to Val and John Tuckwell who made the project possible.

Judith Cook

Introduction

The year is 1586. The place Ireland. Her arms pinioned behind her, a woman stands on a brand-new scaffold especially erected in her honour. Triumphantly organising the show is Sir Richard Bingham, English Governor of Connaught, a man notorious for his brutal treatment of the population and for the savagery with which he puts down insurrections; he has recently hanged a number of hostages as a reprisal for an uprising. He is feeling very pleased with himself for the woman was lured into the trap he had set for her by being offered letters of safe conduct which he subsequently failed to honour. He has no compunction about executing a female prisoner since he considers her to be 'the most notorious woman on all the western coasts, a notable traitress and the nurse of all rebellions in the province for forty years'. She is to be hanged as a warning to others.

The woman in question is Grace O'Malley, variously nicknamed 'Grainne', 'Grainemhaoil' or 'Grania' O'Malley. Though she has been married twice, O'Malley is the name by which she is always known and which she has made almost as notorious as that of 'Bingham', though in a very different way. She is now in her mid-fifties but remains a striking figure. Among the charges levelled against her, apart from rebelling against the English Crown, is that she had been planning to bring in more Scots mercenaries, 'the galloglas', to assist in the latest campaign against the English. She has a reputation for the 'drawing in of Scots', a practice of which the English administration takes a particularly dim view.

One report has it that the rope was actually around Grace's neck when, as the assembled onlookers watched in silence, the sound of a galloping horse was heard and into the crowd rode a messenger from England demanding her immediate release on the orders of Queen Elizabeth herself. Whether or not matters had actually got quite so far, there is no doubt that the planned execution was stopped. Bingham had no alternative but to return her to prison before finally, and reluctantly, releasing her into the safekeeping of her son-in-law, Richard Bourke, known as 'the Devil's Hook', who he rightly rated as little more trustworthy than Grace. Within no time Bourke had joined the rebels and Grace had immediately set about contacting the Scots, arranging to ferry them in using her own fleet of galleys.

But the lead-up to what sounds like a scene from a film or television costume drama had been a long one. Grace's previous career had already spanned trading to the Iberian peninsula and the Mediterranean ports, two marriages, an earlier spell in Dublin Gaol and, most notably, the activity at which she was most successful and for which she had become best known: piracy. She was also a noted gambler, could play at politics and was possibly a part time 'intelligencer' for Elizabeth's spymaster, Sir Francis Walsingham, when it suited her. Today they call her 'the Pirate Queen'.

Yet for a very long time after her death, no mention is made of her in any of the histories of Ireland, not even the Annals of the Kingdom of Ireland by the Four Masters, although there is no shortage of myths and legends, some of which might well be true or at least based on fact. Others, though, have to be treated in a similar way to the apocryphal exploits of Robin Hood or Rob Roy, and for much the same reason. Like them she achieved the reputation of a flamboyant, dashing outlaw to whom such stories naturally accrue with the added spice that in this case it is a woman, not a man, who takes the starring role. However, the attitude of the much later nineteenth-century historians towards her is still distinctly odd. For in some she merits at best only a few lines, and then in connection with one or other of her admittedly colourful husbands, or because she famously publicised the plight of the widows of sixteenth-century Ireland who were legally unable to inherit land. Yet she was a major player in the Ireland of her day. Therefore for accurate, and accurately dated, contemporary information about her various activities, her political involvements and the threat she was thought to pose to the English government, we have to turn to the Calendars of State Papers (Domestic) of the period, the State Papers of Ireland and various reports appearing in the papers of, among others, the Sidney and Salisbury families.

One explanation for the neglect of the predominantly male historians might simply be her gender: she was a woman very much out of place in the man's world of warfare and politics, her behaviour quite outside the boundary of what was considered acceptable even though she lived through an era which saw two Queens on the throne, Elizabeth in England and Mary Stewart in Scotland. But on the whole, although there are legendary exceptions, the Ireland of her day, and later, preferred its women as suffering heroines, preferably *beautiful* suffering heroines. Grace was neither and could swear, gamble, loot and kill with the best of them.

But there might well be other, darker, reasons. She lived at a time of great transition, where the old Gaelic certainties, the very laws, language and customs, were increasingly being encroached upon by the English. It was a time, above all, of shifting loyalties which set province against province, clan against clan, indeed the septs (or tribes) within a clan, against each other. Grace was not alone in changing her allegiances and her attitude to the English towards the end of her life was, to say the least, ambivalent: no easy patriot, she.

So what started out as an attempt to tell the story of the life and times of a highly romantic figure has turned into something altogether more complex. It is also daunting as an English person (albeit partly Celt) to take on the biography of an Irish woman. Nor do I pretend, in spite of a great deal of help, to have been able to get to grips with the immense complexity of the wide variety and scale of the struggles in Ireland during the sixteenth century. For those who want to take this aspect further there are plenty of excellent histories from which to choose, although their authors often disagree . . .

Renowned now in legend, ballad, poetry and even music in her own country, Grace O'Malley remains surprisingly unknown outside it, as I discovered when looking for an interested publisher. What follows will, I hope, bring Grace O'Malley to the attention of a wider audience.

Judith Cook, Cornwall, 2004

1

Momentous and Dangerous Times

Grace was born about 1530, or possibly a little later, making her almost an exact contemporary of the woman with whom the fortunes of herself and her country were to be inextricably bound up. Elizabeth I and Grace were born within a short time of each other and died only weeks apart. Before looking at the state of play between the two countries at the time of their births it is useful to know a little of Ireland's history up to that point. Magnus Magnusson, in his short history of Ireland, *Landlord and Tenant*, puts this well: 'History has been used in Ireland as a *story*, as a rich and passionate source of rhetoric for the next plunge into bitter violence. Perhaps if we all had a greater understanding of how things happened, and why things happened, we might have more sympathy for one another's standpoints'.

Ireland has suffered a host of invaders, starting in prehistoric times with an influx of population, possibly from Brittany. These were the people who built the great monuments of New Grange and Knowth, the stone lines at Carnac in Brittany and the chambered tombs and stone circles found along the west coasts of Britain. Next came the Celts from central Europe who brought with them first iron and the knowledge of how to make it, then Christianity. By the fifth century Ireland was a largely pastoral country, divided into a number of small kingdoms, with a considerable number of monasteries and a strongly established Celtic Christian Church. So strong, in fact, that it sent out missionaries to Cornwall, Scotland, Wales and Western Europe. Marvels accrued to them. Several of this standing army of Irish saints arrived in Cornwall, sailing, legend has it, on leaves, in sieves or by other miraculous means. Others, such as St Columba, appear to have reached Scotland using more conventional means.

In the ninth century the Vikings invaded the country, settling first in Dublin then in Wexford and Waterford. Magnus Magnusson points out that it was this invasion that brought Ireland into the mainstream of European trade and commerce, turning the cities in which they settled into major trading ports. Many of these same trading routes were used from then on by Irish seafaring and trading families, one of the most prominent being the O'Malleys.

So, following the Conquest in 1066, to the Normans. But it was to take them another century before they attempted to annexe Ireland. There was then an influx of land-hungry Anglo-Norman knights, one of the most famous being Richard Fitzgilbert de Clare, Earl of Pembroke, known as 'Strongbow'. They studded the country with their castles and tower houses, some 3000 in all, the tower houses very similar in design to those still to be seen on the Scots/English Border. But it remained a very incomplete conquest, with the bulk of the invaders settling inside what was to become known as 'the Pale', the colonial enclave comprising the counties of Meath, Louth, Kildare and Dublin. The arrival of the Anglo-Normans was to remain a very partial 'conquest', even though some did settle outside the Pale. But while some barons loosely controlled parts of the country, and developed new patterns of trade, they never succeeded in doing what they had achieved in England: creating a new nation that combined the characteristics of natives and incomers alike.

At least some of those who settled outside the Pale were themselves changed and influenced by those among whom they lived, by joint trading, intermarriage and by a growing acceptance of the country's laws and learning. The rest, the descendants of the twelfth- and thirteenth-century settlers who had remained within it, spoke English, accepted the rule of English law and were fiercely loyal to the Crown to whom they looked for protection. The Crown, in turn, counted on their support for whoever was deputised to represent the Crown. These descendants of the Anglo-Norman lords considered themselves to be a bastion against the terrible barbarians outside, not least those in Ulster and along the west coast. They offered protection to their tenants and followers in return for payment and/or military service. But in some instances this in turn could lead to some 'old English' lords getting above themselves, thus becoming part of the problem, rather than its solution. Ireland, by the time Henry VIII came to the throne, was therefore a deeply divided nation. It also had, once one got outside the sphere of English influence, a reputation for being a very dangerous one.

As Francisco Chiericati, a priest and papal nuncio who had toured Ireland, wrote to the Duchess of Mantua: 'Irish people are very religious but do not regard stealing as sinful, nor is it punished as a crime. They hold that we [foreigners] are uncivilised because we keep the gifts of fortune to ourselves, while they live naturally believing all things should be held in common. This accounts for the numbers of thieves: you are in peril of being robbed or killed here if you travel the country without a strong bodyguard. I have heard that in places further north people are even more uncivilised, going about nude, living in caves and eating raw meat'. While Chiericati's notions are a bit over the top, there is no doubt that the politics of the country were chaotic. For those who want more detailed knowledge of the Irish clan families, the law and the politics at the time Grace was born, there are plenty of academic histories available on the subject, but a brief summary can be given here.

At the time of her birth about sixty Irish chieftains (or 'kings' as some preferred to style themselves) ruled their 'counties' or 'countries' outside the Pale quite independent of English rule. Political control, such as it was, rested in the personal headship of the clans, most especially the dominant kin group who were the hereditary rulers of their own and lesser clans. This produced a proliferation of ruling dynasties.

The social system was patriarchal. The lands great or small of the clan leader, the chief, were his property, farmed out to his family and to his tenants. Those living immediately outside his 'country' could also be his tenants, paying him cattle in exchange for having his soldiers on their land as protection. The wives of such chieftains, unluckily finding themselves widowed by warfare or disease, had no rights whatsoever under Irish law to succeed to any of their husbands' lands, an injustice later taken up by Grace even as far as the English Court. Nor did the succession automatically come down father to son but was by election within the extended ruling family. Customarily, such an election took place well before the death of the current chief, the preferred successor being known as a *tanist*. This, theoretically, was designed to prevent quarrels and ensure a smooth takeover of power on the death of the chief (which might well be the case), but all too often by the time the *tanist* was ready to assume the leadership he found there were powerful rival claimants from within his own family. They could be the sons of the chief – even those who were illegitimate but who had been recognised by their fathers – younger brothers, close cousins or members of a different branch of the family altogether.

Unsurprisingly this led, in turn, to internecine warfare and even assassination.

The Irish, the 'Brehon', law was also quite different to that of the English. The word means 'judge' and the brehons were usually hereditary holders of the office. They were experts in the arcane knowledge of ancient legal texts and were called on to adjudicate in cases involving territorial disputes between clans over land or in a variety of matters between individual clansmen. In such cases both parties, if they agreed to ask the brehons to act as arbitrators, had to agree beforehand to their decision. If it was a question of damages, then out of any financial award about an eleventh went to the brehon along with a fee for whichever 'lord' oversaw justice. A successful plaintiff in the case was often forced to seize goods or cattle as a 'pledge for justice'.

But when it came to criminal behaviour the brehon courts were virtually without fixed penalties or punishments. Nor was there any way of enforcing the decision of the courts although traditionally theft, arson and murder were resolved by payments to the victim's family. A convicted thief had to pay back several times the value of the stolen property, a proportion of which went to the chieftain of the plaintiff. The basic principle was that the family was responsible for all its members. Therefore the normal penalty for killing someone, say, during an inter-clan raid or following a cattle-rustling expedition (which in England would be counted as murder) was a special fine known as an eiric which was exacted from the culprit and his kinsmen and was usually paid in cattle, the number varying according to the status of the victim. When a member of the MacCoghlan clan murdered a foster-brother of the Earl of Kildare in 1554, that clan, and the associated Devlins, had to pay the huge fine of 340 cows to the Earl.

Rebellions against English rule and internecine clan

battles resulted in the Irish clans needing substantial numbers of fighting men, more than they could raise themselves, and it is in the thirteenth century that we first hear mention of the *galloglaigh* – the galloglas – who came over from Scotland to fight for the Irish chiefs. The Gaelic name means 'young fighting man'. The galloglas had their own chiefs and leaders whose loyalty was to a particular Irish clan or a lesser clan associated with it, and one of the first Scots to make a name for himself was a MacDonald from Kintyre. MacDonalds were among the most prominent of the galloglas who fought on behalf of the O'Neills in Ulster. The O'Malleys too had their own 'hereditary' galloglas drawn from the Donnell clan. While some of the galloglas finally settled permanently in Ireland, most came over in large numbers from the the Highlands and Islands for the 'fighting season' between May and October, returning home for the winter. There was also some intermarriage between Scotland and Ireland. Shane O'Neill was related by marriage to both the Macleans and Campbells, which was useful when it came to his needing fighting men. Cyril Falls gives as an example the marriage of Tirlagh O'Neill to Lady Agnes Macdonald, widow of James MacDonald of the Isles and the daughter of the Campbell Earl of Argyll. 'This unromantic match between an elderly Irish chieftain who drank like a fish and a middle-aged Scots widow was, from the bridegroom's point of view, a method of obtaining mercenaries, and from that of the bride's relations an insurance policy . . .' The galloglas most closely associated with the O'Malleys were the ClanDonnell, many of whom eventually settled in Ireland.

The galloglas chiefs were accorded great respect both by their own men and the clans for which they fought, and although they are sometimes described as 'mercenaries', this is not how they saw themselves. Traditionally the Irish kerns were the musketeers and the galloglas the pikemen, although there were also some galloglas forces of horse, 'shot', bowmen and halberdiers. When they fought they wore chain mail and steel bonnets but they could look equally intimidating out of uniform. When Shane O'Nell visited London in 1542 he arrived with an escort of galloglas armed, writes William Camden in his *Annals*, 'with battle-axes, bare-headed, with flowing curls, yellow shirts dyed with saffron, short tunics and rough cloaks, whom the English followed with as much wonderment as if they had come from China or the Americas'.

The reward of a galloglas soldier was one bullock per quarter as pay and two for food. The captain of a troop of galloglas was allowed to reckon thirteen 'dead pays' in drawing wages for a band of one hundred, that is, if his company numbered only eighty-seven he was allowed to draw pay for a hundred and pocket the difference.

Cyril Falls, in *Elizabeth's Irish Wars*, writes of the Ulster lord, Tirlagh Luineach O'Neill, having over two thousand men under his command, made up of two hundred 'horse', two hundred galloglas, a thousand kern and four hundred Scots. So who were the four hundred Scots who were not classed as galloglas? They were the redshanks, the true mercenaries, largely drawn from the Western Isles, and hired on what we would call today short-term contracts. They owed no particular allegiance to any Irish clan, did not intermarry with the Irish or settle down in that country, and when they had done what was asked of them and been paid for it, went straight back to Scotland. Legend has it that their name originated from the English who had to fight them and who admired their hardihood in wading through rivers in the winter, which made their legs red ... However, a more sensible explanation is that it was because they wore leggings made from red deer-skin. It was not, says Falls, a term used in contempt, for the English had a tremendous respect for the Redshanks. As we shall see later, Grace made use both of galloglas and Redshanks, and indeed of galleys manned entirely by Scots.

In the early part of the sixteenth century the English kings had taken a fairly relaxed attitude to Ireland, the last major foray – under Richard II in 1399 – ending in humiliation for the English and disaster for him. Then, for a considerable time during the 1400s, England had been taken up with its own internecine power struggles, the long-running civil war known as 'The Wars of the Roses' which finally ended in 1485 with the death of Richard III on Bosworth Field and the triumph of the Tudor Lancasters. To most people, if they thought about it at all, Ireland was a foreign country outside the comparative safety of the Pale.

When Henry VIII succeeded to the English throne he was content, at first, to style himself 'Lord of Ireland', and leave it at that, with only a token presence representing him within the Pale. Up to and immediately following his accession in 1509 the English had been far more concerned about the Scots. By the end of the 1520s and into the early 1530s he had other things on his mind: the prolonged battle to obtain a divorce from Queen Catherine to enable him to marry his mistress, Anne Boleyn, leading, in turn, to the fall of his closest adviser, Cardinal Wolsey; his finally pushing through the divorce whatever the Pope might do or say; the secret marriage to Anne; his subsequent excommunication in 1533 and the birth in that year not of the longed-for son but of yet another daughter, the Princess Elizabeth. A year later he made himself Head of the Church of England and set about 'dissolving' the monasteries, taking their land and wealth either for his own use or to give to his favourites. From outside the country onlookers watched aghast as even churchmen such as the Abbot of Glastonbury or Bishop Fisher were put to death, not to mention Sir Thomas More.

It was shortly after Elizabeth's birth, when Grace would have been about two years old, that he finally turned his attention to Ireland. On bad terms with Spain, France and the Holy Roman Empire and with continuing trouble from the Scots, he realised that over the water was a country which although allegedly under the rule of the English Crown was in reality no such thing. Not only that, the most substantial part of the population remained solidly true to the Pope and the Roman Catholic Church, with close, very close, links with Scotland. He decided to do something about it. After all, if for no other reason, there were yet more monasteries in Ireland which would give rich pickings. Both Grace and Elizabeth had been born into momentous and dangerous times.

2

The 'Crop-Haired Girl'

The O'Malley clan traced their ancestry back to Cosgrach, a descendent of a King killed by the Vikings in 811 A.D., and one of the first references to them appears in the *Annals of the Kingdom of Ireland by the Four Masters.* They described themselves as 'true Gaels', 'Irish of the Irish', and have one of the rare 'O' clan names from which the prefix has never been dropped. At the time of writing, over eighty per cent of O'Malleys still live in County Mayo.

H.T. Knox, in his *History of County Mayo,* one of the very few histories of the area, notes that in the twelfth century *Book of Rights* the O'Malleys had to pay a tribute to the King of Connacht of 100 milch cows, 100 hogs and 100 casks of beer, the King giving them in return 'five horses, five ships, five swords and five corselets'. The clan motto was, and still is, *Terra Marique Potens* – Powerful by Land and Sea. At the time of Grace's birth they held the chieftainship of the baronies of Murrisk and Burrishoole.

Her father was Dubhdara 'Blackoak' O'Malley, the elected chief of his clan, his name generally being given in English as Owen. His septal (or clan) lands were in the west at Umhaill Uachatarach Ui Maille, Murrisk, Co. Mayo, which, again roughly translated into English, became known as the Territory of the Owls. The land stretched around Clew Bay, taking in Ireland's Holy Mountain, Croagh Patrick (still a place of annual pilgrimage), Achill Island and the Corrain peninsula, Clare Island, about four miles out from the mainland, and the islands of Inisturk and Inisboffin. While Clew Bay provides shelter, it is scattered with small uninhabited islets and reefs and can be treacherous. Inland the O'Malley lands were bordered by the Partry Mountains to the east and Maumturk Mountains to the south. Even today, driving from Galway along the 'back road' to Louisburgh and Westport through Leenane and the oddly named Delphi, houses and farms and villages are sparse. The scenery is stunning. Mountains with pointed peaks, like a child's drawing, rise steeply on each side of the valley. Not for nothing has it been described as bandit country.

Writing on Ireland later in the sixteenth century, the poet Edmund Spenser pointed out the difficulties of grappling with a 'flying enemy' in such a terrain, an enemy who 'hides himself in the woods, bogs and mountains from where he will not draw forth but in some strait (sic) passage or perilous ford where he knows the army must pass; there will he lie in wait, and if he find advantage fit will dangerously hazard the troubled soldier. Therefore to seek him out that still flitteth, and follow him that can hardly be, were vain and bootless'. After falling on the unsuspecting English troops or, indeed, members of a hostile clan, the Irish would vanish like smoke into the mountains.

To protect themselves by sea and land the O'Malleys built a chain of castles, not so much out of fear of invasion or to deter the English as protection against other, predatory clans. The principal seat at the time of Grace's birth was Belclare Castle, usefully situated close to a lake with an island to which the family, retainers and fighting men could retreat if the need arose. There were also four more, one near Westport close to the present-day Westport House, another west of Louisburgh, the other two being Kildawnet on Achill Island and that on Clare Island which was to become notorious as the centre for Grace's piracy. Only Kildawnet and Clare Castles still exist.

Most people when they think of castles imagine something on the scale of Chepstow, Raglan, or Edinburgh but most of the Irish 'castles' of the period are quite different, very similar in style to the peel towers of the Scottish Borders: stark, three or four-storey buildings often, like Kildawnet, built in isolated situations commanding sweeping views of land or sea. From the records it appears that Belclare was larger and more spacious than the others. Clare Castle is also slightly different, lower and squatter than most. Its position was ideally suited for piracy, set facing the mainland and so invisible to shipping passing on the west side of the island, yet with a splendid view of the Bay from lookouts posted on the highest point, Knockmore. Clustered close to the tower castles would be the houses or cabins of those who worked either on the land or in some other capacity, almost certainly all clan members. When danger threatened they could take refuge in the castle, along with as many sheep and cattle as could be accommodated. No trace of the houses survives but it is known that they were often built of stone, with a thatched roof. An archaeological drawing suggests they were circular and, in style, not unlike the Iron Age houses of the West of England built over a thousand years earlier.

The O'Malleys were very wealthy in terms of cattle and sheep and were also expert fishermen. But they did not suddenly discover piracy with Grace, they already had a long and notorious history of piracy by sea and raiding on land. *The Annals of the Four Masters* refer to an early O'Malley who went with three ships full of fighting men to Killybegs in County Donegal, fell on the inhabitants in the middle of the night, burned the town and took many prisoners. Also to Tuathal O'Malley who in 1413, returning home from some unspecified mercenary foray to Ulster, was blown with six of his ships on to the west coast of Scotland. All of them were wrecked, over two hundred of his men were drowned and he barely escaped with his life. What Grace did was to carry on and improve the tradition, adding to it what amounted to a protection racket.

The Annals provide much of what we know of early O'Malley history with the glaring exception, as all modern commentaries point out, that nowhere does Grace figure in any of them. A fifteenth-century poem translates as:

> They are lions of the sea,
> Men acquainted with the land of Spain,
> When seizing cattle from Kintyre,
> A mile by sea is only a short distance for the
>   O'Malleys.

They were so unpopular in the city of Galway that bylaws were brought in to keep them out. Galway, by the efforts of its own citizens, was one of the most successful trading ports of its day and aimed to keep it that way. It was described by Oliver St John in 1614 as a small town 'but all of faire and statelie buildings. The front of the houses (towards the streets) are all of hewed stone uppe to the toppe ... in a uniform course as if the whole towne had been built upon one model'. Unsurprisingly, Galway felt it could do without competition from outsiders and in 1518 a special by-law was enacted fining any citizens who welcomed and entertained such people as the O'Malleys on feast days without the permission of, and a licence from, the mayor and council, so that they should not 'strutte nor swagger thru the streets of Galway'.

Galway's dislike of the O'Malleys was as much to do with their legitimate trading interests as with their piracy, for their trading was in direct competition with the merchant venturers of Galway. From the thirteenth century Ireland was exporting wool, grain and hides and by the end of the 1400s also flax, furs and salted fish. The O'Malleys traded, not only with ports in England and Scotland but as far as the Baltic, Flanders (the Flemish were the principal importers of hides), Spain and Portugal. Also, it would seem from later accounts that they ventured into the Mediterranean as well. Like other Irish traders they brought back salt, wine, spices, fine cloth and other luxury goods.

Much is made throughout Grace's life of her great fleet of galleys, vessels propelled by a single sail and up to thirty oarsmen, and there is little doubt that they were ideal for piracy as they were nothing like so dependent on the wind to get them out of trouble or manoeuvre into a good fighting position as conventional vessels using only sails. They were also useful for ferrying galloglas over from the west coast of Scotland.

But galleys would not have been particularly suitable as trading vessels and the earlier O'Malley fleet, and that of Grace, must have included vessels such as caravels or carracks. Confirmation of the sturdiness of such vessels came in 2002 when the almost complete remains of just such a one was found under the silt of the Usk Estuary outside Newport in Wales. The boat is eighty feet long by twenty-five feet wide and has been dated to the winter of 1465 when the English were busily engaged in the Wars of the Roses. From damage to the mast and some of the timbers, it is thought it ran into the Usk estuary to shelter having been damaged in a storm. It is only now being excavated but was found to have been carrying a wide range of goods including jars of different kinds and cloth, which suggests that its cargo was very similar to those imported by Galway merchants and the O'Malleys.

Whatever type of trading vessels the O'Malleys sailed,

however, it is certain they bore little resemblance to that patronisingly suggested by H. V. Morton in his *In Search of Ireland:* 'No one knows the composition of her [Grace's] fleet. She must have possessed certain wooden vessels but no doubt the bulk of her navy was composed of coracles . . .'

We know from contemporary English records of the massive increase in foreign trade throughout the sixteenth century. By the mid-1550s English traders had forged strong links with the Levant and were also regularly visiting Algiers, Alexandria, Aleppo, Venice and Zante. Zante belonged to Venice and was the centre of the currant trade, another popular import. It is reasonable to assume that the Irish followed suit.

This, then, was the clan into which Grace was born. Her mother, Margaret, was also an O'Malley from another branch of the clan, after which the situation becomes somewhat confusing as Grace officially described herself as being the only child and 'sole heir of her mother'. But there was also an O'Malley son, Donal. It could be that Owen had a wife before Margaret, but it is more likely that Donal was the son of a woman with whom he had a liaison but did not marry. In earlier times under both Irish and Welsh law a 'recognised' son born out of wedlock had the same share to the rights and the family fortune as a legitimate one. Some accounts suggest that Grace almost literally elbowed her brother out of her way, one story going so far as to say that 'like Hatshepsut of Egypt she calmly set him aside and declared her intention of becoming chief of the clan', but this is patently nonsense. Not only would it have been impossible for her to make such a demand, Donal was still alive and well and living on his father's lands as late as 1593.

We do not know exactly where or when Grace was born but most likely it was at Belclare. It is difficult to describe what the interior must have been like since nothing of it remains, but we know from the tower castles that it is likely to have been very dark, with at most perhaps one or two small windows on the top floor and only slits in the walls below. However, the family quarters would have been fairly comfortable, the walls hung with hides or even wall hangings and the rooms decently furnished with tables, benches, cupboards and bedsteads. From the remains of Clare Island Castle it is possible to see that there were fine stone fireplaces on every floor, from the kitchens up to the chief's apartments on the highest level. There were also 'slop holes' set in the walls for sanitary purposes.

As the daughter of a major chieftain Grace had a privileged if hardy childhood with plenty of servants to see to the family's needs. Travellers describe visits to such households where the wife of the chief would act as hostess and welcome them to the family table where they would be feasted and entertained by harpists. No doubt Grace was expected to learn from her mother how to run such a household when she married. The family ate well. Sheep provided mutton, and the cattle not only beef but milk for buttermilk (popular with rich and poor alike), butter and cheese. There was also game, poultry and plenty of fish, corn, oats, barley for bread and porridge and plentiful green vegetables such as cabbage. No doubt much of it was washed down with the wine imported from the Iberian peninsula but there was also ale and the O'Malley lands were famous for the honey-based mead. There was even *uisce beatha*, whiskey.

There are repeated English reports of the Irish of the time living in squalor, the men and women alike clothed in little more than rags and a 'blanket' (similar to a plaid), but we also know from contemporary reports that this was certainly not true of the better off. In records of the time the men are described as wearing trews, or sometimes 'pleated skirts', linen shirts and the ubiquitous 'blanket', the women long chemises to their ankles, laced bodices, pleated skirts and 'rolls of linen on their heads'. These rolled head dresses varied in design in different parts of the country, much like the linen and lace coifs of Breton women.

In the summer, when times were peaceful, the entire household would move to the summer pastures on the mountains, taking with them their sheep and cattle to graze them on the uplands, a practice known as 'booley-ing'. At its best it would be something of a holiday, a time for relaxation, and there are jolly prints of feasting chieftains sitting at long tables in the open air listening to a bard or harpist. One wonders how often the weather was that kind. But they had to be on their guard, for during booleying both men and cattle were vulnerable to attack by the rustlers of neighbouring clans and, later, to foraging English soldiers.

One thing we do know and that is that by the standards of the day Grace had a good education. She was taught Latin and spoke it fluently enough to be able to hold her own in later years, not only with government envoys in Ireland and ministers in England but eventually in discussions with Queen Elizabeth herself. In England it was only the women of the English nobility, or the daughters of academics such as Sir Thomas More, who were taught such a skill. The girls born into artisan families were lucky if they learned to read or write. Grace was probably taught by a priest, for it was not uncommon for priests to act as tutors to the sons of the chieftains, though how often this stretched to educating daughters we do not know. For years a form of Latin remained familiar to much of the Irish population, not least because of the Latin Mass, and there are accounts of the language being used, most unexpectedly, by shopkeepers, ordinary townsfolk and even young country lads, when speaking to foreigners.

The martyred Jesuit priest, Edmund Campion, wrote snobbishly in 1571: 'Without either the precepts or observations of congruity the Irish speak Latin like a vulgar language, learned in their common schools of leachcraft, and law whereat they begin their children'.

Living so far away from Dublin and hemmed in by mountains, the O'Malleys were remote from most of what was going on not only in England but also within the enclave of the Pale. All that was about to change. Previously Henry VIII had handed the overseeing of Ireland to Cardinal Wolsey. But Wolsey had died almost immediately following his fall from grace, after which Henry's interest became far more personal even though he was still deeply involved in the problems caused by his divorce of Katherine of Aragon and subsequent marriage to Anne Boleyn. Indeed Anne's father, whom he had made Earl of Wiltshire, was now one of his group of advisers on Ireland who were pressing him to appoint Sir William Skeffington as Lord Deputy there.

It was then, in 1535, that, spurred on by the schism with Rome, Thomas Fitzgerald, son of the Earl of Kildare, rebelled against the Crown and played right into Henry's hands. The revolt was put down by Skeffington with the utmost ferocity. Among the atrocities committed in the aftermath was the execution of all forty survivors of the siege of Maynooth Castle who had surrendered in good faith. Their fate came to be known as 'the Maynooth Pardon', i.e. being put to death. The words 'Lydford Law' were later to acquire a similar notoriety in England following the Monmouth Rebellion.

Nor were the leaders of the rebellion spared. Thomas himself, having done a deal with his uncle-in-law Lord Leonard Grey, who had been appointed marshal of the King's army in Ireland, was imprisoned in the Tower and his life spared, but his five uncles, including two who had actually been on the King's side and one who was neutral, were taken to London and executed at Tyburn, after which sixty-seven of the others involved were also put to death.

Henry then seriously set about putting his stamp on the country. From now, he declared, he would officially become King of Ireland and in 1541 an Act was brought in to that effect. It had become necessary, it stated, 'for as much as the Irish men and inhabitants of the realm of Ireland have not been so obedient to the King's Highness and his most noble progenitors, and to their laws, as they of right and according to their allegiance and bounden duties ought to have been. Wherefore at the humble pursuit, petition and request of the lords spiritual and temporal, and other of the King's loving, faithful and obedient subjects of this his land of Ireland, and by their full assent, be it enacted, ordained and established by authority of the present Parliament, that the King's Highness, his heirs and successors, Kings of England, be always Kings of this land of Ireland, to have, hold and enjoy the said style, title, majesty and honours of King of Ireland ... as united and knit to the imperial crown of the Realm of England'.

The Bill came before the Irish Parliament, the handful of representatives of the Pale and pro-English landowners, on 26 June. They responded with grovelling sycophancy to 'their only protector and defender under God of our realm' and 'most willingly and joyously consented and agreed to the same'. Their loyalty had been assisted by the fact that Henry had bribed some of the Irish lords to support his claim, by officially giving them their own lands in perpetuity, along with titles, although hitherto they had not personally owned the lands but held them on behalf of their own clan. Commenting on the event in *Landlord and Tenant – A View of Irish History*, Magnus Magnusson points out that clan fealty was replaced by crown feudalism. The year 1541 was to prove a crucial one in Irish history.

Nor did it stop there. A further Act was brought in 'for the English Order, Habit and Language'. No person or persons, it declared, 'shall be shorn or shaven above the ears, or use the wearing of hair on their heads like unto long locks called "glibes", or have or use any hair growing upon their upper lips, called or named a "crommeal", or use or wear any shirt, smock, kerchief or linen cap coloured or dyed with saffron, nor yet use or wear in any of their shirts or smocks above seven yards of cloth to be measured according to the King's standard'. It goes on and on in the most extraordinary detail. No women must wear or use any 'Kyrtell' or coat tucked up, or embroidered, or garnished with silk, 'nor couched nor laid with ornaments after the Irish fashion', and no person or persons were to use or wear any mantles, coats or hoods made after the Irish fashion.

Having comprehensively dealt with hair styles and clothing, Henry moved on to the Irish language. 'And be it also enacted that every person or persons, the King's true subjects inhabiting the land of Ireland, of what estate, condition or degree he or they be, or shall be, to the uttermost of their power, cunning and knowledge, shall use and speak commonly the English tongue and language . . . and shall bring up his or their children in such places where they shall, or may have occasion to learn, the English tongue, order and condition'.

All this was necessary because Ireland, Henry had realised, was becoming a threat on the international stage. It had remained true to the Catholic faith and to Rome. It had strong sympathies with both France and Spain and long-standing, strong and increasing ties with Scotland. Suddenly he found himself with a vulnerable western flank.

If the O'Malleys were becoming aware of the gathering storm, then they showed no sign of it, continuing to wear what they wished, speak the Irish language, practise the brehon law and make no effort to offer their submission to the Crown of England. They also continued trading. At the time the Acts were passed Grace would have been around nine or ten years old and it was about then that she acquired the nickname Grainemhaoil, Graine Uaile or Graine Mhaol (all forms have been used, and others besides). Grainemhaoil is a corruption of the Irish form of Grace – Grainne – but it also means bald or crop-haired. There is no true record of how she came to be given it but every folk tale, legend or account of her life tells the story of how, when still a child, she pleaded with her father to take her with him on his ship which was about to leave with a cargo for Spain. Her mother told her not to be so foolish. Girls didn't go to sea like common sailors and she was also a chief's daughter.

Furious, she ran off only to reappear later in boys' clothes, having cut off her hair, thus acquiring the nickname and persuading her parents to let her go. Given her subsequent career, which included foreign trading as well as piracy, there might well be some truth in it and that she learned her undoubted seafaring skills from her father. If this was indeed the case it would be interesting to know what Owen O'Malley made of his two children, for it was his crop-haired daughter who accompanied him on his ventures while his only son, known as Donal ni-Piopa – Donald of the Pipes – presumably stayed at home and played the flute!

3

Bride to the Ferocious O'Flaherties

Owen O'Malley and his family also spent time in their castle on Clare Island. It is sparsely populated today but there is ample evidence of earlier settlements dating back five thousand years, and as late as the mid-nineteenth century some 1700 people were living there. As well as the castle, the O'Malleys had founded an abbey back in 1224. It was originally a Carmelite cell dedicated to the Holy Virgin but by the time Grace was growing up the original cell had grown to a substantial church with its own domestic buildings and had been taken over by the Cistercians at Knockmoy. The outbuildings have long gone but part of the church remains including the chancel, on the ceiling of which can still be seen the remains of remarkable mediaeval paintings dating from the thirteenth century, showing men on foot and on horseback, a harper and a variety of animals including a dragon, birds, trees, stags, and a cockerel.

On one of the walls there is also a slab, elaborately carved with a rearing stallion, a wild boar transfixed by arrows, and a galley, under which is the name 'O'Maille' and the family motto, *Terra Marique Potens* (Powerful on Land and Sea). Next to it is a tomb. Tradition has it that slab and tomb mark Grace's grave but recent archaeology suggests the tomb is much earlier, and the slab later, than the dates of Grace's life. What the ruins also show is that the abbey survived the Dissolution of the Monasteries for a considerable time.

The trips back and forth to Clare Island would have introduced Grace early to the hazards of Clew Bay and its tides, currents and reefs, and it is likely that it was then she acquired her first knowledge of boats. It is certainly reasonable to assume that she did indeed learn her trade from her father. Seamanship cannot be acquired merely by reading books, even if any such had been available to her. It has to be practised and there would have been precious little time or opportunity to learn the essential skills from scratch when she was a young wife and mother in the years before she took to piracy.

We admire today's single-handed sailors, especially the women, but at least they, like all those who go to sea today, have the benefit of radar, echo sounders and constant radio and satellite communication. The seafarers of the mid-sixteenth century were assisted only by the compass and the marine astrolabe used to calculate and fix the position of the stars; that is, when they were visible and not concealed by cloud, fog or rain. For the sailors of the day the world was still flat and somewhere, frighteningly, there was an edge over which one could topple. Indeed they were still coming to terms with the fact that the earth moved round the sun and not the sun round the earth, hitherto considered to be the centre of all things, for Copernicus's work on the subject was not published until 1534. Nor had anyone as yet discovered how to work out longitude. It is almost impossible to imagine the skills needed then, not to mention knowledge of wind and weather on which the survival of the vessel and all aboard depended.

For another three centuries or more shipwrecks following bad weather were a commonplace, especially on the treacherous west coasts of Ireland, Scotland and Cornwall. All too easily a vessel making for port could find itself embayed, blown in to a bay on a lee shore from which there could be no escape, and the O'Malleys had to face the possibility every time they put to sea. They have also been accused of being wreckers but it is unlikely that they deliberately set out to entice passing ships on to the rocks any more than the Cornish who have a similar reputation. There was no need: given the perils of the coastline, it was unnecessary. The O'Malleys like their Cornish counterparts would strip a wrecked vessel of its cargo and valuables, accepting it as 'the bounty of the sea', particularly when times were hard.

The suggestion sometimes made that Grace's skill and seafaring prowess are largely mythical, nothing more than the stuff of folklore and legend, does her a disservice. Admittedly it is hard to find records of women who feature in history as valiant seafarers but there is at least one: Mary Bryant, the daughter of a master mariner from Fowey in Cornwall who was transported to Botany Bay for highway robbery, organised a daring escape in the Governor's boat. During the subsequent weeks at sea she spent much of her time navigating and steering it through uncharted waters, often in appalling weather, until the escapees made a perfect landfall at East Timor, a distance of over 3000 miles. This feat of navigation was later described by Captain Bligh, who knew a thing or two about the subject, as the greatest ever voyage in an open boat. Mary Bryant's expertise at least is on record in a statement given later by one of the convicts who escaped with her.

If Owen sailed regularly to Spain and Portugal, let alone into the Mediterranean, then his ships would have had to be armed against possible attack from privateers and pirates sailing out from the Iberian peninsula, not to mention the Barbary pirates of the North African coast. We know from later records how well Grace handled the latter and Owen must have taught her how best to deal with such an eventuality, maybe even by direct experience. It was the kind of knowledge that would stand her in good stead later when the lives of herself and her crew were at stake.

Trading voyages were not pleasure cruises. A captain also required many other skills, apart from seamanship. Sailing ships, of necessity, were crammed with men and it is almost impossible to imagine when looking at a replica of the *Santa Maria* and *The Golden Hind* what it would have been like to be confined in so small a space. Quarrels were sparked out of nothing and every man carried a knife. Discipline was essential and strictly enforced. Grace would learn how her father handled his crew, how he kept them from quarrelling and fighting. Nor would she be under any illusions about what life on board ship entailed: it was hard, without basic comforts, lacking even basic privacy, although Grace would have shared the captain's quarters with her father. On arrival at a foreign port she would watch how he haggled over the price for his own cargo and for whatever he might be taking back with him. She also picked up other talents most unsuitable for a well brought-up young girl, later becoming notorious for her gambling and swearing,

But however proud Owen might well be of his tough, lively daughter, there was never any question of her continuing in the family business. Her duty, her place in life, was to make the best possible marriage and to that end, when she was about fifteen, Owen began looking for a suitable husband for her.

The world was not standing still as Grace learned her seamanship. Hard on the heels of the two Irish Acts, Henry brought in other measures. He wanted to abolish all traditional Irish titles such as 'the O'Neill', indeed he wanted to do away with the 'O' prefix altogether. He also stepped up the implementation of the policy already mentioned, that which became known as 'surrender and

re-grant', that is the encouragement of the Irish chiefs
to make formal submission of themselves and their lands
to the Crown in exchange for receiving them back as
estates-intail in perpetuity along with a title. In the early
days there was little enthusiasm among the chieftains,
and even some of Henry's advisers warned him that it
might have the reverse effect to that intended. 'Believe
me with my experience,' Sir Henry Blount told him, 'the
titles and honours do rather weaken then strengthen
them [the chiefs] in this country.' But in the event Henry
and his successors were to be proved right.

In 1542 Henry's fears that Ireland posed a real threat
to the stability of England were dramatically confirmed
when a number of Irish chieftains went to Scotland and
offered King James V the Irish crown. This is one of
those intriguing 'what ifs?' of history. What if James had
accepted?

But James had no ambition to become King of Ireland,
he had more than enough to cope with at home. He had
come to the throne as an infant, following the death of
his father on Flodden Field, and was brought up in
dramatic circumstances, his childhood precarious,
ending with a daring escape from Edinburgh and his
enemies. His was a complex character. On one hand he
could be the man of action, capable of great brutality,
on the other a conscious role-player, sometimes wander-
ing the countryside in disguise, pretending to be a simple
farmer. This did not, however, as John Prebble points out
in *The Lion of the North*, fool anyone, 'the commonalty'
being known to shout out 'there goes the King of
Scotland!' when they came across him. Ironically the
practice led to his being remembered as 'the Poor Man's
King', when in reality he was famously extravagant. He
remains notorious on the Borders for having invited John
Armstrong of Gilneckie in Eskdale, chief of one of the
great reiving families, to a reconciliatory feast by way of

a 'loving letter'. Armstrong arrived with his men only to find that the invitation was a trap. James hanged the lot of them.

When he decided to marry, he wanted a French bride in order to strengthen the Auld Alliance. He also needed a woman with a large dowry. His first attempt foundered when he took a good look at the woman in question but then Francis I offered him his daughter, Madeleine. James agreed, married her, and brought her back to Scotland only for her to die within two months. Eager to ensure the French connection and learning that the husband of Mary of Guise had recently died (and that she had turned down an offer from Henry VIII on the grounds that she had only one neck), he quickly married her by proxy and she was duly delivered to Scotland.

The Irish chieftains had not chosen their moment well. James was rapidly acquiring a reputation as a greedy, brutal womaniser increasingly isolated from his barons whom he excluded from his councils. His motives for agreeing to meet King Henry in York in 1542 remain unknown, but whatever they were he never kept the appointment. What ensued was disaster. Whether it was the snub to Henry, the knowledge that the Irish chieftains had offered James the Irish crown, the desire to teach the Scots a lesson once and for all or a combination of all three, Henry resurrected the old claim to the Scottish crown. The end came on 24 November 1542 with the Battle of Solway Moss.

Abandoned by many of his lords, his army unwilling, James left before the battle even started, leaving his men to face Sir Thomas Wharton, deputy warden of the March, and 3000 English troops. The Scots were driven on to Solway Moss to perish either by sword and arrow, or to drown in the marshland or the waters of the Esk. After leaving his army to its fate, James went first to Linlithgow where his wife was in the late stages of a third pregnancy. The outlook for the child's survival was poor for they had already lost two baby sons, then, increasingly ill, he went on to Falkland Palace. He died of unknown causes on 14 December at the age of thirty-one after learning that his Queen had been safely delivered of a daughter.

The reason for recording these events at some length is because of the role that infant princess was destined to play in the politics of the sixteenth century, known for all time as Mary, Queen of Scots. In 1542 the future Queen Elizabeth was nine years old and for the next ten would be fighting not only for her political survival and place in the succession but for her life. The outlook for her infant cousin was equally uncertain. Meanwhile Grace O'Malley, who was to earn the title of 'the Pirate Queen', was learning the necessary skills from her father. The lives and fortunes of Mary Stewart and Grace could hardly have been more dissimilar but what they did have in common was that both, in their different ways, would prove to be thorns in the side of the English government for the best part of fifty years.

At the end of the day Owen did not go far afield for a bridegroom for Grace. He settled on a member of the O'Flaherty clan whose vast tracts of land bordered his to the south. The O'Flahertys were famous for their belligerence: 'the Ferocious O'Flahertys' whose motto was *Fortuna Favet Fortibus* ('Fortune Favours the Brave'). However, they lived peaceably enough with the O'Malleys and indeed had often been their allies in local wars.

The chosen bridegroom, considered an excellent catch, was Domhnall-an-chogaich O'Flaherty, Donal of the Battles. He was a warlord, the son of the chieftain of a sept, chief in his own right of the barony of Ballinahinch and, more important still, the elected *tanist* or successor to the chieftainship of the entire O'Flaherty clan. The advantages of such a match were obvious.

The O'Flaherty lands took in almost all of what is now Connemara, out to the mountains known as the Twelve Bens and almost to the edge of Lough Corrib which stretches away towards Galway city for thirty miles. Donal's main castle, which was to become Grace's new home, was in an isolated spot on the coast at Bunowen, near to Slyne Head. Owen could reasonably congratulate himself on contracting a marriage which pleased both families.

Whether or not it pleased Grace was irrelevant. But it is unlikely that even young as she was she imagined any weight would have been given to her own preference, let alone that her marriage would be a love match. Romantic love did not come into it. Her future role was fixed on the day she was born: to make her husband a good wife, run his household efficiently and bear him strong, healthy children. If it turned out that the man in question was also attractive, lively and caring, then that was her good fortune. If he wasn't, then too bad.

The wedding most likely took place in the church of the second abbey the O'Malleys had founded earlier, close to the shores of Clew Bay and to Croagh Patrick, of which only the ruins now remain. There would have been much feasting, drinking, music and dancing, after which Donal took his sixteen-year-old bride back to his castle. In reality Grace was not all that distant from her family, but to reach her new husband's lands meant a detour round the deep inlet of Killary, Ireland's only fjord, then through miles of difficult terrain to the westernmost tip of Connemara.

As befitted her station in life, Grace brought a considerable dowry to her marriage, certainly cattle, horses, sheep and household effects, possibly even gold. Although Ireland considered itself a good Catholic country, its attitude to marriage was liberal to a degree, at least among the nobility and landowners. According to Dr Mary Lyons of Trinity College, there were no fewer than seven categories of 'wife' and five of 'concubine' at that time. However, the most strict form of marriage, such as that entered into by Grace and Donal, had set rules. Even if the contract made at the time was not a written one, her rights were made clear in the event of her being either widowed or divorced. The latter seems surprising but Irish marriage law even allowed for divorce.

In either event, Grace would receive her dowry, or its full value, back. What she could not do was inherit any of her husband's land or property, something she was to complain about forcefully over the years, even going to the length of petitioning the Queen. In fact the widow of an Irish chief or major landowner did not even have the right of her English sister to a lifetime's interest in the lands and property of her husband. Indeed in England it could go a good deal further, for we know that Shakespeare's maternal grandfather, Robert Arden of Wilmcote, left his substantial farm and lands to Shakespeare's mother, Mary, who was not only a daughter but also the youngest of his six children. The idea behind the Irish system was that clan land belonged to the entire clan, and such a law made for stability. However, in spite of this being the case, Grace is also on record as stating her own mother did actually own land in her own right.

To say that Grace's life changed drastically is an understatement. Taken from her familiar family home and a life spiced with trips to foreign ports, she suddenly found herself, a very young wife, living in an isolated fortress among people she is unlikely to have known well, if at all. We know very little about Donal except that he seems to have had no interest in anything whatsoever except inter-clan warfare: not for nothing was he nicknamed 'Donal of the Battles'. We do not even know his age in relation to that of Grace.

She would have had to grapple with the running of a castle with its servants, soldiers and possibly other family members, a daunting task for a woman a good deal older than a teenage bride. As to other matters, the sex life of herself and her husband leaves much to the imagination. One wonders if Donal even felt he had the time to take off his body armour and his boots before pleasuring his wife, or simply clanked into the bedchamber as he was. All we know is that she gave him three children in quick succession, two sons, Owen and Murrough, and a daughter, Margaret. After that there were no more. No doubt she felt she had done her duty by providing two male heirs and a daughter who could be traded in marriage as she had been herself.

Certainly Donal seems to have left Grace to her own devices as he pursued his long-standing feud with the Joyce clan. No doubt his views were conventional for a man of his time and he assumed that everything was as it should be: he went off to fight possibly for weeks at a time, while his wife was fully taken up with the affairs of the household and the bringing up of his children, dutifully welcoming him home when he deigned to return. But we know that it was nothing like enough for Grace, for within a few years of her marriage she had set out on a course of action which would put her right outside the boundaries of what was considered remotely appropriate behaviour for the wife of an Irish chieftain; a course which would lead to her being described in English State Papers years later as: 'The most notorious woman on all the western coasts, a notable traitress and has been nurse of all the rebellions in the province in forty years'.

4

Revenge and Piracy

In 1549, about two years after his marriage to Grace, Donal had been involved in a very shady episode indeed which might explain why from then on he has such a low profile in local affairs. It is a story worthy of one of those late Elizabethan or Jacobean plays like Webster's *The White Devil* in which the plot involves the activities of a murderous brother and sister. Donal's sister, Finola, was married to David Bourke of the MacWilliam clan of Mayo. He was the elected tanist to the overall chief of the clan with every prospect of eventually becoming 'the MacWilliam'. Finola bore him a son, Richard, but Bourke had been married before and already had another and older son, Walter, who was his designated heir.

Therefore Finola, jealous of her stepson's prospects and unable to see any possibility of changing the situation, invited her brother to the Bourke castle of Invernan, west of Galway city, and explained what she had in mind. Taking a role similar to that of Lady Macbeth, she persuaded Donal to murder Walter so that her own son, Richard, would become his father's heir and therefore possibly the next tanist to the MacWilliam himself. The couple were sufficiently clever about it for there to be no absolute positive proof that they were behind the killing of Walter, but there was never any doubt in the minds of those living at the time, or those who have looked into it since, that Donal did the deed and that his sister was the instigator. The murder of Walter Bourke certainly added to Donal's already doubtful reputation and there is little or no record of his playing much of a role in his clan's affairs thereafter.

Finola's son was always known as Richard-an-Iarainn, 'Iron Richard'. Sources differ as to whether this referred to his personality, a fondness for his suit of armour which he took everywhere with him, or because there were plentiful deposits of iron ore on his lands. Ironically that same Richard was later to play a major and quite unforeseen role in Grace's future.

Details of the next few years of Grace's life are hard to come by and largely based on tradition, folk tales and legends. Some of the stories do have the ring of truth, others are more likely to be apocryphal. But in a land where storytelling was, and still is, an art it is reasonable to assume that there is at least a core of truth in those which have lasted down to this day, even if they have been embellished over the years. Also until news of her activities begins to appear in State Papers, dating proves a difficulty. If, as is generally agreed, she married Donal about 1546/7, it would have coincided with the death of Henry VIII in 1547.

He was to be followed by his sickly son, Edward VI, who, in turn, was succeeded by his half-sister, Mary Tudor. The Reformation had continued under Edward VI but scarcely with as much zeal since those acting on his behalf spent more time fighting each other than looking to the affairs of State. Two new protestant bishops were chosen to spread the word in Ireland but for neither would it prove to be a fortunate honour. One died before he was able to take up his new post while the other, John Bale, ended up being chased out of the country following the accession of Mary in 1553.

In England, Mary's reign is remembered chiefly for the persecution of so-called heretics, the dreadful burnings at the stake in Smithfield and the market squares of provincial towns which earned her the title 'Bloody Mary' by which she is still known. But in Ireland her reign was a brief time of respite, a breathing space before the accession of Elizabeth who would change everything forever.

Under Mary, the Lord Deputy of Ireland, Sir Anthony St Leger, was charged with the restoration of the Catholic rites of the Church 'as of old times used' even though he had been prepared to push through political and social changes of a different nature under Edward VI. Edward had decreed that the Book of Common Prayer and its forms of service should be in Ireland as they were in England, and St Leger had done as he was told but he had been as conciliatory as possible about it and few bore him any ill will. Now he was pushing at an open door. The restoration of the Catholic faith and its form of service was wildly popular with rich and poor alike. Almost immediately Mary had appointed a number of Catholic bishops and the country's relationship with the Pope went back to what it had been before Henry declared himself Supreme Head of the English Church. Cardinal Reginald Pole, now Papal Legate to the English, was also made Legate of Ireland. Unfortunately time proved to be short but a few brief efforts were made to counteract the dissolution of the monasteries, the priory of the Knights Hospitaller of St John was restored and St Patrick's church in Dublin was re-established as a cathedral. The triumphant culmination of the change of policy and religion was the marriage of Mary to King Philip II of Spain. In part it was Philip who encouraged Mary to make examples of heretics; however, unlike their unfortunate counterparts in England the protestants in Ireland did not suffer persecution for their faith. For a short time, therefore, the Irish outside the English enclaves could breathe easy – not only a Catholic Queen on the throne of England but a Queen married to one of the most powerful monarchs in Europe.

The respite Mary's reign provided gave Grace the perfect opportunity to establish herself in her new calling. The O'Flaherties were not as famous as the O'Malleys for their seamanship though the position of Donal's castle with its deepwater anchorage suggests that it was made use of and that they did have a number of vessels; no doubt Grace added to the fleet over the years. Certainly, one way or another, she succeeded in acquiring a force sufficient to become a real threat to merchant shipping making its way past Slyne Head en route for Galway city, as was noted in the Carew State Papers of about that time. So concerned were the Galway city councillors that they wrote to the English administration in Dublin complaining of the continuing 'roads used by the O'Malleys and O'Flaherties with their galleys along our coasts, where they have been taking sundry ships bound for this poor town, which they have not only rifled to the utter overthrow of their owners and merchants, but have most wickedly murdered divers of young men to the great terror of such as would willingly traffic . . .'

Throughout her career Grace called the type of piracy that she practised 'maintenance by land and sea'. In actual fact it amounted to a protection racket. Just as the Border reivers, who gave us the term 'blackmail', would fall on some hapless village or hamlet, offering the inhabitants the option of either paying them a fee in money or cattle and accepting their protection, or being killed, their homes burned and their cattle stolen, Grace gave the captains of ships coming into Galway a similarly stark choice: either they paid her a toll in goods or kind or she would blow them out of the water. If they decided to make a fight of it, then she had a boatload of clansmen and galloglas to back up her threat.

There is no record of what Grace looked like, apart from a somewhat catty note in a letter dated October 1582 from Sir Nicholas Malby to Queen Elizabeth's spymaster, Sir

Francis Walsingham. In it he tells Sir Francis that he had met recently with 'Grany O'Mally' who 'thinks herself no small lady'. Knox, in his history of Mayo, when discussing Grace, writes that the real Queen Maeve of Irish history bears as much resemblance to the beautiful and legendary Queen Maeve of folklore 'as Grace O'Malley of nineteenth century legends to Grainne ni Maille of the sixteenth century, the legendary Grace becoming chief of the mighty Clan O'Malley and visiting Queen Elizabeth as a sister sovereign'. To make up for the lack of any description, there are the 'interpretations' and 'artist's impressions': the Maureen O'Hara lookalike complete with big hair, billowing sleeves and thigh boots who has apparently just stepped out of a 1930s Hollywood pirate movie; a 1793 print of what the meeting between Grace and Queen Elizabeth might have looked like, both women almost equally well-dressed and portrayed as being a good deal younger than they actually were at the time; an eighteenth-century rendition showing Grace standing, apparently pointing into the wide blue yonder, and dressed in the kind of gown, complete with décolletage, as worn by those taking part in a ballroom scene in a television production of an early nineteenth-century costume drama.

Since tradition has it that she took a string of lovers in her youth, it is reasonable to assume that she was not unattractive to men, though power can also prove enticing. As to clothing, then obviously clambering around sailing ships in all kinds of weathers, let alone taking part in fights, would make breeches a great deal more practical than long skirts.

Tradition also has it that Grace did not only turn to piracy during those years but also began trading in her own right to the foreign ports she had visited with her father, very often captaining such voyages herself. She also regularly provided ships to ferry redshanks and galloglas over to Ireland from the west coast of Scotland and throughout most of her career had a substantial army of galloglas of her own, mainly composed of McDonnells. But she also played a further role in the affairs of the O'Flaherties. It is generally agreed that during the later years of her married life she became, in all but name, chief of her husband's sept of the O'Flaherty clan. Whether it was because Donal was not trusted by his people, refused to recognise his responsibilities, was always away fighting or simply a numbskull, Grace took hold of the reins apparently without opposition. There would be disputes to settle, decisions to make, seeing to the collection of the rents of the twenty-four towns in the area and much else besides. Since she is also credited with stirring up rebellion from that time on, she must also have been politically active though it is often difficult to discover exactly what part she did play.

The breathing space of Mary's reign was short-lived In November 1558 Mary died, finally accepting that what she had been carrying inside her was a tumour, not a pregnancy, and that she would never have been able to bear Philip a child. So it was that against all the odds the twenty-five-year-old Elizabeth finally succeeded to the throne. Although the new Queen was to declare – and indeed she adhered to this for some considerable time – that where religion was concerned she did not seek 'windows into men's souls', within three weeks of her becoming Queen the Acts of Supremacy and Uniformity were back on the Statute Book and she automatically became not only Queen of Ireland but supreme governor of the Church in Ireland.

She could hardly have inherited a more hazardous situation where foreign affairs were concerned. Mary Stewart, now sixteen years old, had spent the previous ten years of her life at the French court affianced to the

Dauphin, while her mother remained in Scotland facing both an onslaught from the English (culminating in the Battle of Pinkie) and years of bitter internal strife; not to mention the arrival on the scene of John Knox, bringing with him his own form of protestantism. Shortly before Elizabeth's accession Mary finally married the young Francis. A year later King Henry II was dead, Francis became King, and Mary, briefly, Queen of France. Elizabeth therefore began her reign with the two great European powers of the day ranged against her. Philip II would never forgive the English for the way he felt he had been treated during his brief marriage to Mary Tudor, while the marriage of Mary and Francis made the link between France and Scotland stronger than ever, a Scotland with a major wrong to avenge.

Religion apart, the policy of grant and regrant in Ireland or, as it was also known, of submission and regrant, was reinstated with vigour. The policy was designed to encourage (or later force) the great clan chiefs to surrender their lands to the Crown in exchange for Letters Patent re-granting their lands back to them again on the understanding that if they were then disloyal their lands would be forfeit, but if they remained loyal, then they would be left alone. To encourage this the chiefs were often bribed with a title but what the English administration appeared to be unaware of was that the chiefs did not own 'their' land, it was owned by the whole clan. It was hardly surprising therefore that the policy caused bitter divisions among clan members.

The history of the politics, wars and rebellions in Ireland during the second half of the sixteenth century is of a complexity almost impossible to disentangle. Alliances among the Irish formed and broke, even with clans, as did those between the Irish and the English. There was no guarantee that a chief who had accepted an English title, along with ownership of clan lands, would always remain loyal to the Crown, and he would be almost as likely to rebel as one of the diminishing numbers of chiefs who had not accepted submission and regrant. Some chieftains changed sides several times within one short period. Ireland truly was a land of war. To put Grace O'Malley's story in context it is only possible to use a broad-brush approach here and explain the various rebellions and warfare as they affected it.

In 1560 a new Parliament met in Dublin to confirm the Queen's title and the reintroduction of the protestant religion; almost immediately there was real trouble in the form of Shane O'Neill, son of Con O'Neill. Shane was an adventurer who needs a book to himself. His father had visited Henry VIII's Court at Greenwich back in 1542 and been persuaded to give up the hereditary title of 'the O'Neill' in exchange for the belt and sword of an earldom. Henry made him the Earl of Tyrone. Con also agreed that he and his people should from then on 'use English habits', acquire 'a knowledge of the English language, practise tillage, build houses, obey English law, and hold his lands by knight service'.

His successor under the new English system would automatically be his eldest son, Matthew, but Shane, though younger, was the elected tanist to his father under the old Irish laws. It was never to be put to the the test, for the unfortunate Matthew was mysteriously waylaid on the road and killed before the situation could be resolved, after which Con O'Neill, now an old man, was forced to flee for his life and seek refuge within the Pale. He died shortly afterwards and Shane immediately claimed the old title of 'the O'Neill' under Brehon law at a ceremony held at the Rath of Tullahogue in east Tyrone, where the traditional recognition of a new chief customarily took place. As Shane himself put it, all the lords and gentlemen of Ulster assembled and 'by one assent . . . they did elect and choose me to be the O'Neill and by that name did they call me'.

He also had a colourful private life. He divorced his first wife to marry a second, then wanted to go on to a third and at one time suggested he might marry the Lord Deputy's sister. He also had a number of concubines. The new Queen was therefore faced almost immediately with a rebellion on her doorstep. Shane began to raise an army. There had, hitherto, been no such thing as a standing army attached to any clan and the tradition was that only freemen could bear arms. Shane was to change all that. He conscripted his peasants, arming them with swords and spears, and augmented these by bringing 1500 redshank Scots over to join him, among them Campbells, McLeans, MacLeods and McKays from Kintyre and Islay. By the middle of the year his men were rampaging almost at will, pillaging and burning on the very borders of the Pale.

Thomas Radcliffe, Earl of Sussex, who was Lord Deputy of Ireland under Queen Mary, had been kept in the post by Elizabeth. Shane was proclaimed a rebel and a traitor and Sussex, with what army he could muster, marched north from Dublin in 1561 and occupied the town of Armagh in Ulster. But as many other military commanders were to discover to their cost, the Irish proved elusive; 'lacking the encumbrance of towns', wrote Sussex, 'guarded by woods and bogs and mountains and retaining much mobility the Irish were hard to dominate'. Nor would they do the decent thing and stand and fight, he complained, but running from bush to bush, firing on the enemy all the time, 'they hold it no dishonour to run away'. Who came out of it best during the succeeding months depends not only on which contemporary accounts you read but which version is accepted today by the various historians, both English and Irish, who have written on the period.

What is beyond argument is that Shane was persuaded to visit London in 1562, arriving, as was described earlier, complete with a train of wild galloglas. What promises were made to the other on either side of the English-Irish divide are also open to debate; neither trusted the other and both would later renege on what was supposed to have been agreed. The English would soon be fighting Shane again but for a brief while there was relative peace and the English withdrew from Armagh.

Meanwhile, taking advantage of the general unrest, Richard-an-Iarainn Bourke, he whose step-brother had been murdered by Grace's husband, set out with a force of a thousand galloglas to rob and plunder the neighbouring lands of the Macmaurices, close to Galway city, provoking another section of the Bourke/Macwilliam clan, headed by the Earl of Clanrickard, to engage 'Iron Richard' in battle, killing seven hundred of his men. Richard left the field and fled for his life to the relative safety of County Mayo. But the general unrest had finally turned the attention of the English to the clans of the west coast who had not made any attempt to submit themselves to the English Crown. So it was that the O'Flaherties were finally drawn into the net.

As early as 1560 a minor O'Flaherty chieftain, known as 'Murrough of the Battleaxes', began to expand his influence from his power base in the town of Oughterard close to Lough Corrib and started raiding the territory of Conor O'Brien, the Earl of Thomond, who raised an army to march against Murrough. To reach him Thomond travelled through Clanrickard country to Galway, 'opposed by some few citizens', and continued on through Joyce country. Murrough promptly retreated into what is described as his 'fastness' and Thomond, considering further pursuit too perilous, turned back. For the next few years Murrough had everything his way until in 1564 the Earl of Clanrickard, determined to prevent Murrough's incursions into his own country, undertook another expedition against him with a considerable number of troops.

Murrough again retreated, whereupon the Earl 'took prey of the whole country', helping himself to whole herds of cattle which his people then drove on towards the pass at Galway en route for Clanrickard's lands. But they were swiftly pursued by Murrough who overtook them at Trabane (the White Strand) about two miles west of Galway, and in the ensuing battle Clanrickard's forces were defeated. A contemporary account states: 'The earl's people were forced to turn their backs and the most part of them drowned in the sea and river of Galway . . . some got over the river but such was their apprehension of death, they knew not how'.

Murrough obviously had to be stopped but, loathe to spend money on more expensive military excursions, the English government astutely offered him a pardon in exchange for his agreeing to submission and regrant. Murrough weighed up the advantages and agreed, promising to observe the Queen's peace thereafter. He was duly made the overlord of all Connaught, in effect 'the O'Flaherty'.

But under brehon law the O'Flahertys already had a chief, Donal Crone, waiting to take up the office, and Grace's husband Donal was his elected successor. It made no difference and both men were ousted. There followed many months of internecine warfare, intrigue and double-dealing within the O'Flaherty clan, 'Sir Murrough' triumphing in the end. It was a classic case of divide and rule. Taken up with their own internal struggles, the O'Flahertys had little inclination to fight the English and never proved a serious threat again. Not only that, the English had achieved a major goal, a foothold in the west of Ireland.

One account says that Donal and his father were fight-

ing with the MacWilliams against the English as late as
1570, and this might be so of Donal Crone but by that
time his son had been dead for some years, although there
is no official record of exactly when he died. Throughout
the Shane O'Neill rebellion and that of Sir Murrough,
Donal's time was still taken up with his bloodfeud with
the neighbouring Joyces. A major bone of contention
over the years was the right to a castle on an island at the
head of Loch Corrib. After fierce fighting Donal finally
took it, earning himself a new local nickname *Donal an
Acullagh*, Donal the Cock, for his prowess in the field
and arrogance afterwards. The castle became known
thereafter as Cock's Castle. But his triumph was short-
lived. At an unknown date in the early 1560s the Joyces
took their final revenge on Donal, tracking him down
and killing him while he was out hunting. They then
turned their attention to re-taking their castle.

Possibly Grace had actually joined Donal in his newly
acquired property, remaining there in the time immediately following his death, for certainly strong tradition
has it that when the Joyces arrived with their forces, Grace
was firmly ensconced inside with her own men and that
she defended Donal's prize so fiercely that the Joyces
finally gave up and went home. This has the ring of truth
for the castle has been known as *Caislean-an-Circa*, Hen's
Castle, ever since.

There is a further story concerning Hen's Castle: that
immediately afterwards the English laid siege to it while
Grace was still there, calling for her to surrender immediately which she refused to do. That she had the lead
stripped off the roof, melted down and then poured over
the battlements on to besiegers has the ring of truth in
such a situation. There are similar stories told of doughty
women whose husbands were away fighting and who
found themselves under just such a siege during the
English Civil War. What rings less true is that Grace had

no boats on the island to enable her to escape. For someone whose prime activity required the use of waterborne craft it seems hardly likely that she would have allowed herself to be marooned in Loch Corrib in such a vulnerable position without a boat of some kind, or more than one. In any event we are told that she sent one of her clansmen to the mainland – did he swim? – to light a beacon on nearby Doon Hill, thus summoning her followers to her aid, after which the English were successfully defeated.

But however brave Grace was, however good she had proved as an administrator and whatever she might have brought to the O'Flaherties by her seafaring activities, with the death of Donal it was all over. There was no point in staying where she was, for she could inherit neither land nor property. Given that Sir Murrough was now officially the chief of the whole clan, the possibility that either of her sons, now presumably in their late teens, might be elected overall chief as their father had expected to be, was remote. Sometime in the early 1560s, therefore, Grace returned to her father's land in Owls, leaving her sons behind and, very possibly, her daughter. There, at the very least, she would inherit some land of her own through her mother. All she could officially take away with her was the value of the dowry she had brought to Donal as a sixteen-year-old bride.

But in fact she took a great deal more than that, for when she left for Mayo, a substantial number of the O'Flaherty clansmen and galloglas went with her.

5

The Pirate Queen

Grace's parents were still alive when Grace returned to Mayo, as was her brother, Donal of the Pipes, the family presumably still based in Belclare Castle. From every point of view therefore it was practical for her to settle in the castle on Clare Island. It gave her independence and an ideal base for piracy, enabling her both to consolidate her power base and extend it further. During her years in Bunowen Castle, close to Slyne Head, she had operated roughly from Killery in the north to the entrance to Galway city harbour. At the end of the 1560s, by which time she had married for a second time (of which more later), she is credited with having virtual control of the sea lanes along almost the entire west coast of Ireland and even beyond. In the north her galleys regularly visited Kintyre, her control over the narrow sound between Achill Island and the mainland enabling her to sail north without needing to round Achill Head. In the other direction her men were boarding ships as far south as Wexford. No vessel was safe from her galleys, not even those from Spain.

Her range of operation gave her a unique perspective on the amount and type of shipping using the west coast of Ireland, and later there is some evidence that this would be put to a highly controversial use. She suffered remarkably little opposition, the owners of the merchant ships making their way to and from Galway city and beyond apparently accepting the situation, preferring to pay her a toll and ensure safe passage rather than make a fight of it. She was also prepared to provide pilots for a fee to those who fell into line, a valuable service given the hazards of Ireland's Atlantic coast. At any one time she had several hundred men at her command. As well as O'Malleys and the O'Flaherties who had gone with her to Mayo, she also attracted dissident members of other clans, including Conroys and MacNalleys, along with the Clandonnel galloglas, boasting that a crew of Conroys and MacNalleys were better than a ship full of gold.

It is impossible to over-estimate her achievement. She had flown in the face of convention in every possible way. Apart from the myths and legends of Irish warrior queens there was no precedent for what she achieved as a woman in a man's world. She had married a supposedly 'strong man', who was prepared to fight anyone at the drop of a hat and expected easily to keep a wife in order, yet had then embarked on a major career of piracy. Furthermore she had also, in effect, acted as chief of that sept of his clan. For her husband's clansmen to have sufficient confidence in her abilities to accept her as their captain at the start of so dangerous and chancy a venture is almost beyond belief. That she retained their continuing loyalty and remained in control of them whatever the circumstances suggests that she had a truly charismatic personality. But even that would have been insufficient had she not earned their respect by proving herself a master mariner, a brilliant strategist and, above all, successful. Repeatedly we are told of her men's admiration and loyalty, men who saw her at close hand every day. She lived with them, fought with them, was prepared to put her own life at risk, and in the intervals between fighting she gambled with them, swore with them and, tradition has it, slept with any of them that took her fancy.

It was during her time at Clare Island that she became

known as the Pirate Queen. By the time her father died (date unknown) she had established members of her family in every strategic point around Clew Bay and was also gaining notoriety for her activities on land. There is a report in the Celtic Studies Department of University College, Dublin by Maire Ni Neill who was told when she visited the Aran Islands in 1944 that 'there was a great battle fought between the people of Aran and Grainne Ni Mhaille. Her people came in ships to Port Mhuribhe [Kilmurvey Bay] and the battle raged east to Cill Einne. Grainne won'. She attacked a whole series of castles including that of O'Loughlin in the Burren, close to Galway, and Renvyle, knocking down part of its walls with cannon balls fired from her ship. When the people of the island of Inisboffin complained of her activities she promptly impounded their boats even though the island came within the jurisdiction of the O'Malleys.

There then comes a strange interlude. It is during this period that Grace allegedly fell in love. There are several versions of the story but the common ground is that she was on a 'pilgrimage' to a holy well on Clare Island on St Brigid's Day. There are two holy wells on the island, but as both are within easy walking distance of Clare Castle this hardly suggests a major excursion involving mortification of the flesh, as does the ascent of Croagh Patrick even today. While she was at the well, one of her lookouts brought news of a wreck off Achill Island. In spite of the fact that the weather was bad, with gale-force winds, Grace duly set out for Achill in one of her vessels spurred on by the prospect of plunder from a rich wreck, but by the time she reached Achill the ship had been driven on to the rocks and smashed to pieces. However, among the wreckage and bodies washed up on the shore she found a survivor.

His identity remains in doubt. He is variously described as a Norwegian, a Scot and 'Hugh de Lacy of Wexford'.

In any event, whoever he was Grace took him home to Clare Island and they became lovers. We are not told how long the idyll lasted, possibly only months, for Grace had made too many enemies, among them a sept of the MacMahon clan. The MacMahons were major players in the politics of sixteenth-century Ireland, and on maps of the time most of their lands are shown inland and well to the east of the O'Malleys. But there was also a sept of the clan based on the north side of the River Shannon, close to the estuary, and presumably these were the people Grace had offended, possibly by extracting toll from their ships or raiding their property. In any event the MacMahons bided their time then tracked down Grace's lover while he was deer hunting in Achill and killed him. If this is true, then hunting in the west of Ireland in the sixteenth century was obviously a hazardous business, since we know Donal is supposed to have met a similar end. It could be, though, that the stories became confused with each over the centuries.

However, whether he was hunting or not, the MacMahons took the opportunity when it presented itself to murder him. Grace's retribution followed swiftly and a tale which began with a pilgrimage also ended with one. She learned that the MacMahons were making a pilgrimage to tiny Caher Island, a relatively short distance to the south of Clare Island, though whether it was actually possible, as is claimed, for her to have seen them sail by and land there is doubtful given the distance, and since presumably they were sailing up from the south. At any event she set off with her men, first capturing their boats so that they were unable to escape, after which she killed those who had slain her lover. Still not satisfied, she then sailed on to their stronghold at Donna Castle and took it by force.

But during the years she was establishing herself as the scourge of the west coast of Ireland, events were rapidly moving on in Scotland and England. Grace was no fool and she must have realised that while Mayo had so far managed to avoid the attentions of the English government, this was a situation which was unlikely to last much longer, given what she would have learned of events in Scotland and the reaction to them in England. Regular trips to Kintyre would have kept her abreast of what was happening in that country. The position was that while she may have had power in her own right, as a woman on her own, a widow, it was unlikely that the English would be prepared to negotiate directly with her. However much she might dislike the idea, she needed an alliance with another strong man, preferably one with plenty of land. She therefore determined to marry again; as events turned out, it proved to be a wise decision.

We left Shane O'Neill, flushed with the success of his visit to London, returning home having promised to deal with 'the robbers from the Hebrides'. Having got himself off the hook, however, he was in no hurry to do this but turned instead to Scots nearer home. As well as the redshanks who came over for the brief fighting season and those galloglas who might remain for months or years, increasing numbers of the latter were settling permanently in Ireland, particularly in the Glens of Antrim. Shane decided therefore to launch an attack on the MacDonnells, presumably members of the same clan (although differently spelt) that had been involved for so long with the O'Malleys.

The most powerful MacDonnells of the time were James and his brother, 'Sorley Boy', sons of Alexander MacDonnell, Lord of Islay and Kintyre and great-great-grandson of John Macdonald of the Isles. Sorley Boy, like Shane, was a chancer and he had already spent time in an English gaol. On his release he and James had forced the nearby MacQuillan clan to acknowledge them as overlords, t is giving the MacDonnells virtual control of the nort eastern corner of Ireland. Their territory, viewed fro Ulster, seemed a prize indeed.

Shane f t attacked Sorley Boy at Coleraine and was beaten of although Sorley Boy was badly wounded. Shane th. retreated for a while to give himself time to raise mor troops, but in 1565, once he felt he had sufficient force at his disposal, he marched into Antrim. Thoroughly alarmed at the prospect before them, the MacDonnells lit beacons on Torr Head as a signal to summon their kinsmen to come from Scotland to assist them, but by the time the reinforcements arrived Shane had captured the MacDonnells' castle at Red Bay and 'bracke it to the grounde rather than the Skotts should again enjoy the same'. The two armies met up on 2 May 1565 at Glenhesk, a fight described as 'bloody and furious', but at the end of the day the O'Neills had won, they had captured eighteen ensigns and thirteen banners, James and Sorley Boy were taken prisoner and seven hundred of their men lay dead. James, badly wounded, was carried away from the field to an O'Neill stronghold where he died of his wounds. Sorley Boy was taken off first to Dunsverick Castle which belonged to the O'Neills and then on to the MacDonnells' own castle of Dunluce, an almost impregnable rock fortress. When at first those inside refused to surrender, Shane told them he would starve Sorley Boy for every day that passed without their giving themselves up. After three days they surrendered, unable to face the prospect of allowing their chief to starve to death.

This was the height of Shane's career. He had now acquired by conquest an even greater portion of Ulster, but in doing so had made himself bitter enemies, enemies who would not rest until they had their revenge. He might well for now have broken the power of the Scots in Antrim but was almost certain to pay the price for it himself later. The English government, looking on, found the situation deeply satisfying. It could well be that Shane's activities would kill two birds with one stone.

In 1560, within two years of his marriage to Mary Stewart, Francis I was dead and immediately a hitherto secret clause in her marriage contract made Mary a direct threat to the English Crown. It stated that should she die childless, then both the Scottish throne, and her right to the succession to that of England, should revert to the French.

On 14 August 1561 Mary sailed for Scotland to a country very different to that which she had left. The death of her mother had left in its wake a complex political situation and the country was now in the hands of Protestant lords. As a result Mary's first Mass on home ground caused a riot. Once again she became a useful counter in the game of European politics, and almost immediately efforts were made to find her another husband. Suggestions included the archduke Charles of Austria (the Pope's choice) and Don Carlos (the son of King Philip II of Spain). Elizabeth even sent her own favourite, and possibly lover, Robert Dudley, Earl of Leicester, up to Edinburgh as a suitor in spite of the fact that he was under suspicion of murdering his wife. Negotiations with all of them dragged on until, quite suddenly, Mary made up her own mind and determined on Henry Stewart, Lord Darnley, son of the Earl of Lennox and Margaret Douglas, granddaughter of Henry VIII. Darnley was handsome in a weak, boyish kind of way but had little else to recommend him except his own faint claim to the throne of England.

From first to last the marriage was dogged by scandal, from the murder of Mary's secretary, David Rizzio, organised by conspirators including Darnley, a murder which took place in front of her when she was heavily pregnant, to Darnley's own dramatic death in what we would call today a terrorist outrage. In spite of the dreadful ordeal of watching Rizzio's murder, Mary had successfully given birth to a healthy son, but there was talk of a divorce. Then Darnley fell ill with smallpox. Mary had him taken to a small house on the outskirts of Edinburgh at Kirk o' Fields and it appeared there had been a reconciliation between the two of them, Mary spending a considerable amount of time at his bedside. Then on 9 February 1567, after talking with him 'pleasantly' during the evening, Mary left the house to go to a party. In the early hours of the morning the house was blown up and Darnley was found dead. He had escaped the explosives only to be strangled in the garden. Controversy rages to this day: whether or not Mary was in on it remains one of history's unsolved mysteries.

Across the Border, the Queen and her government looked on appalled. Mary, a honeypot for men, was now back again in the marriage market, but even this paled into insignificance before the fact that Mary had provided Scotland with an heir and therefore, if Elizabeth, as was looking increasingly likely, did not marry and have children of her own, a future King of England. It went from bad to worse. Whether by force or inclination, Mary became the lover of the Earl of Bothwell, the person most closely implicated in the Kirk o'Fields murder, marrying him only three months after Darnley's death. The lords had had enough. She was seized, taken to Edinburgh, and forced to sign an Act of Abdication making her son James the King. Imprisoned afterwards in a castle on an island in Loch Leven, Mary escaped, crossed the Solway and threw herself on the mercy of her cousin Elizabeth. She was literally on Elizabeth's doorstep and from now on she was to prove the Queen's Achilles heel.

In 1566 Elizabeth had installed a new deputy, Sir

Henry Sidney, as Lord Deputy of Ireland with a brief to bring in those clan chiefs who had still not submitted themselves to the Crown. Sidney did not trust Shane O'Neill an inch, even though he had represented his defeat of the MacDonnells as service on behalf of the Queen. From Sidney's own writing it is clear he became obsessed with Shane O'Neill, seeing him as a personal enemy and the greatest single obstacle to bringing the entire northern province under English rule. He made half-hearted attempts to do a further deal with Shane but got nowhere, reporting back that 'Lucifer had never been more puffed up with pride and ambition than O'Neill', who had bragged that he 'never made peace with the Queen but by her own seeking'. Sidney built garrisons along Shane's border and began to reel in the vassal chiefs, including the MacMahons, with promises of favours to come. Finally, when it looked as if it was going to come to a major fight, Shane made overtures to his old enemies, the MacDonnells, offering their chief, Alexander Og, the release of Sorley Boy (whom he still held imprisoned) in exchange for assistance against Sidney. Alexander appeared to agree and Sorley Boy was duly released. But Sidney sent a Captain Piers to Alexander offering him a deal: he would secure on the MacDonnells in perpetuity the clan's settlements in the Glens of Antrim in exchange for their assistance.

It soon became obvious what that assistance was. The official spin on Shane's death was that it was accidental and occurred during a drunken brawl. The MacDonnells had invited the O'Neills to a feast at which sack and whiskey flowed like water. Eventually a quarrel broke out between Shane and one of the MacDonnells in the course of which he was fatally stabbed. In actual fact it was a set-up, most likely on the direct instigation of Sorley Boy acting on Sidney's behalf. Certainly the drink flowed freely but Shane and his immediate followers were brutally knifed to death. His head was 'pickled in a pipkin' and sent to Dublin Castle for display over the gate.

Sidney was briefly replaced in his post by Sir William Fitzwilliam, returning again in 1571, by which time the Pope had famously excommunicated Queen Elizabeth under the Papal Bull *Regnans in Excelsis*. It absolved all good Catholics from any allegiance to the Queen of England and declared open season for would-be assassins, and there, standing in the wings, was her Catholic successor, Mary Stewart.

Roughly about the time of Shane O'Neill's death Grace finally made her choice. Love, affection, possibly even respect did not enter into the matter. It was a purely pragmatic decision. It was also a choice rich in irony, for her new husband was none other than Richard-an Iarainn Bourke, that very same 'Iron Richard' whose step-brother Donal had murdered to enable him to become the likely successor to the chief of his clan. Thus Finola, Donal's sister and Grace's sister-in-law, became her new mother-in-law! Richard was still more or less hiding out in Mayo, but had acquired a reputation as a hard man. Knox describes him as 'a plundering, warlike, unjust and rebellious man who continually wore his armour' – which suggests the couple shared at least plundering and rebellion in common. Richard had either been married before or had taken concubines for he had three sons, Edmund, Walter and John, and a daughter Catherine, though it is more likely that they had been born in wedlock and that he was a widower. He was also illiterate, extant material relating to him showing that he was only able to sign necessary documents with his mark. Grace's move was a shrewd one. Richard-an-Iarainn was now chieftain of a sept of his clan and still the principal contender to become 'the Macwilliam', the chief of all the Bourkes. It was also geographically sound, for the Bourke lands bordered those of the O'Malleys to the north and were extensive and would provide Grace with further bases along the coast to the north. So it was generally agreed to be a good match. But this time the bride was no longer a young girl destined for an arranged marriage and from the start she laid down the ground rules. It was to be a trial marriage, a secular union of the kind which remained legal in Ireland until as late as 1603. The agreement was for 'a year and a day' or 'one year's certain', at the end of which either party could call it off.

There are various stories about what happened at the end of that year. According to H.V. Morton, 'Grace, it is said, insisted on observing what the Americans regard as the latest thing in unions, a companionate marriage. If, after twelve months, the marriage was not satisfactory, either party to it should have the power to dissolve it. Some reports say that she employed the companionate year in garrisoning her husband's strongholds along the coast, and at the end of it closed the gates of her castle upon him and declared the marriage ended'.

Another story tells of Richard rolling home from the wars to find his doors barred against him and Grace up on the roof of Carraigahowley (Rockfleet) Castle from which she shouted down 'I dismiss you', thus bringing an end to the marriage. It is a good story but if indeed she did so, then she must have changed her mind as we know from the Calendars of State Papers that she remained married to Richard until his death.

She had one very good reason for remaining married to him, for although by this time she was at the very least into her thirties, middle-aged by the standards of the day, about a year after her marriage she bore Richard a son. She called him Tibbot, Theobald in English, and he was known thereafter as *Tibbot-an-Long*, Tibbot of the Ships. He was manifestly her favourite, very much the cow's calf, and from the beginning he also shared her love of seafaring. There are several variations on the story that is told of the circumstances surrounding his birth.

It is said that towards the end of her pregnancy and against all advice Grace insisted on captaining a trading venture to the Middle East. In some accounts the subsequent event takes place the day after Tibbot's birth, in others the same day. The fullest version appears in Volume II of *Ordnance Survey – Letters Containing Information Relative to the County of Mayo*. Grace, we are informed, was 'generally called Graine na glearbach, or Grace of the Gamesters, so called from the many professional gamblers she always had about her'. The versions of the story vary as to whether those who attacked her ship were 'Turkish corsairs' or 'Barbary pirates', but in any event such an attack took place somewhere off the Iberian peninsula and in this account the attackers are Turks.

At first Grace remained in her bed while fighting raged above her on deck until the captain of the vessel came below to inform her that they were losing the battle, suggesting she might come up on deck as this would help rally the men. Whereupon 'she replied: "May you be seven times worse this day a twelve month if you cannot do without me for one day!" Then, springing out of bed with all the vigour of a convalescent heroine and throwing a blanket about her, which she fastened with a string about her neck, she took a brace of blunderbusses and appeared on deck dancing and capering about to attract the notice of the enemy. The Turkish officers being struck with surprise at the gigantic size and strange figure of the Queen of Umhall, assembled together to laugh at her. This was all she wanted for she stretched forth both her hands and fired the two blunderbusses at the officers exclaiming "Take this from unconsecrated hands", alluding to her not having been "churched", for it was then, and still is, the belief in Umhall that a woman is unlucky and calculated to destroy the fertility of rivers and to blast the fruits of the earth until she is churched and purified.

'She killed all the Turkish officers by the heavy slugs she scattered among them, after which the Turks, being dismayed at the animation of her presence and at the loss of their officers, she easily captured their ship, led the sailors captive, and hanged them all at the castle of Carrigaholt.'

It is very likely that all the stories are apocryphal, although De Burgo, writing later in *Hibernia Dominicana*, reported that Tibbot acquired his nickname because his father, Richard, the invincible warrior, had by the widow Grania O'Malley of the O'Flaherty family 'the knight Theobald-ni-lung, that is of the ships', because he was born at sea.

There is another legend told of this favourite son. Grace called her three sons to her and gave them each a seed to plant as they pleased. Owen and Murrough planted theirs in good soil, in prepared ground and, from when the first shoots appeared, nurtured them until they reached maturity. But Tibbot threw his into the sea. Months later Grace asked her sons what had happened to the seeds. The elder two told her how they had planted them and that they had now produced strong and healthy plants. Tibbot, however, told her that he had thrown his into the sea 'for I set mine in the deepest and most fertile soil of all'. To which Grace replied 'You are my son'. Myths and legends they may be, but such tales no doubt helped enhance the reputation of a seafaring son born to a famous seafaring mother.

6

'Iron Richard'

Although Richard-an-Iarainn's main residence was his castle at Burrishoole, it was another Bourke property, Carraigahowley Castle (now known as Rockfleet), a few miles further north along the coast, that Grace chose as her base for her various activities. Rockfleet remains closely associated with her to this day. From the main road between Newport and Achill, a narrow lane winds down to the head of a creek on Clew Bay to where the tower castle stands, a lonely sentinel, looking out over a seascape which cannot have changed since Grace stood on its ramparts looking out to sea.

Unfortunately, although a faded notice on the wall claims that a key is obtainable to allow a visitor to look inside, for safety reasons this is no longer possible. Anne Chambers, who visited Rockfleet in the early 1970s without any let or hindrance, described what it was like inside. The tower had four floors, a spiral stone staircase winding up to the main living quarters on the fourth floor which was paved with stone flags. As in Clare Castle, there was an elaborate fireplace, this one with stone seats. An arched doorway, above a drop of fifty feet, suggested to her that it might have been a loading bay for hoisting provisions up to the living quarters from the landward side, but it might also have done duty as a window, as those clearly visible from the outside are little wider than the loophole slits used for muskets. A privy or *garderobe* on the seaward side saw to sanitary needs. From the top floor a further staircase led on to the ramparts above.

What makes Rockfleet famous is the special loophole in the south wall through which, so tradition has it, the hawser of Grace's favourite ship was passed and then firmly tied to the bedpost so that she would know at once if an enemy tried to steal it while she was asleep. The interiors of all the tower castles both in Ireland and Scotland look pretty bleak, but no doubt when they were occupied the walls would have been whitewashed or hung with wall hangings and fires would roar in the fireplaces. Since Grace traded in luxury goods, no doubt she enjoyed displaying examples of what she brought back with her.

But comfort was not of primary importance. From the ramparts of Rockfleet it would be possible to see anything and everything entering Clew Bay from the open sea and any intruders making their way to it by land. It was from Rockfleet that she organised her 'maintenance by sea and land' of the west coast of Ireland.

As must now be obvious, the situation in Ireland in the 1560s was complex enough quite apart from English expansionism as individual septs of a clan fought among themselves, one clan fought against another and alliances formed and broke with frightening rapidity. The same applied to many of the agreements between the Gaelic Irish and the English government to whom Ireland was a hydra-headed monster. No sooner had deals been settled, submission and regrant accepted and titles handed out than one or other of the arrangements would break down, an apparently 'loyal' lord or chief would rebel and a part of the country thought to have been more or less settled would once again burst into flame.

Nor did the feuding stop in the island of Ireland. The Earl of Sussex, the first Lord Deputy of Ireland, and the second, Sir Henry Sidney, were bitter and ambitious rivals, both seeking to enhance their reputations, one constantly denigrating the other. Each had used every possible stratagem to solicit the Queen and lobby for the post. This was the period early in Elizabeth's reign when pacifying Ireland looked like a fast track to fame, fortune and further preferment, a post from which the successful candidate fully expected to return to London crowned with glory. Later in the century after years of bitter experience it was seen for what it was, a poisoned chalice, the short straw, portray it how you will, not unlike today's post of Minister for Northern Ireland, described recently by one ex-incumbent as 'the graveyard shift'.

Both noblemen came up with long-term schemes for governing the island, neither considering it necessary to consult with any of the interested parties. The Queen approved both schemes in turn but the lucky candidate for the post was immediately faced with a major obstacle: while her priority was to extend English influence as quickly as possible, Elizabeth wanted it done without any cost to the Exchequer. As both men were to find out, Sidney at increasingly disenchanted length, official support vanished like snow in summer as soon as money was involved. However difficult this proved for the Lord Deputy and his officials, it was even tougher on the men serving under them. From the 1560s until the end of the century the lot of the English soldier was a hard one. A memo in the *Calendar of State Papers* dated 15 July 1573 notes that the English soldiers in Ireland were now over two years behind with their pay.

The position was no better twenty-two years later when a similar note dated 13 March 1595 pointed out the lack of money and victuals for the men and that 'much needless suffering was inflicted upon them', partly through the parsimony of the government and partly through official corruption in Ireland. The Bishop of Chester, writing to Sir William Cecil, now Lord Burleigh, told him that a popular proverb in Chester was 'it is better to be hanged at home than die like dogs in Ireland'. So whoever accepted the post was faced with the constant nightmare of lack of money and resources. The hope that the collection of rents and taxes of various kinds from the chiefs and newly created aristocracy would make the administering of Ireland financially self-sufficient proved a vain one.

As the first Lord Deputy, Sussex's method of dealing with the Irish had been to press on vigorously with submission and regrant and put down any sign of revolt by military means, showing no mercy. There is no shortage of reports in State Papers over the next forty years of rebellions being crushed, revolts put down, after which everyone remotely involved, including women and children, was 'put to the sword', 'hanged' or 'executed'. Sidney could be, and often was, just as ruthless as Sussex but he also came up with other ideas. Rebellious chiefs, for instance, would not be given the opportunity to submit to the Crown but would have their lands confiscated and parcelled out and given either to loyal chieftains or Englishmen who wanted to settle in Ireland. Such a policy would also bring in revenue.

Then came another innovation. In 1569 Sir William Cecil persuaded the Queen to appoint two 'presidents' for the provinces of Munster and Connaught to serve under the Lord Deputy, each province to have its own council. The man chosen for Connaught was Sir Edward Fitton who was formally installed in his post by Sir Henry Sidney in person. But, as Cyril Falls puts it in *Elizabeth's Irish Wars*, 'the unfortunate man found that he had entered a wasps' nest, which he was ill advised enough to stir with a stick, beginning by burning what he was pleased to call "idols" in the province's churches'. R. Bagwell in *Ireland Under the Tudors* is less kind, describing Fitton not so much as unfortunate as 'an ill-tempered quarrelsome man, not at all fitted for the delicate duty of turning Irish into English order'.

His appointment almost immediately produced the reaction it was supposed to prevent. In 1570 his tactless and destructive activities prompted the Earl of Thomond, who was also chieftain of the O'Brians' country (now County Clare), to come out in open rebellion. He was soon joined by the O'Rourke in Leitrim. Thoroughly alarmed, Sidney persuaded the Earl of Ormond to come in on the other side. It was at this point that the Bourke clan, and indirectly Richard-an-Iarainn and Grace, were caught up in events, for 'the MacWilliam', Shane Oliverus Bourke, clan chief of the Bourkes, gave his support to the Earl of Thomond, bringing with him a large number of clansmen and an even larger number of galloglas, mostly Clandonnells who also fought for the O'Malleys. There were several skirmishes, followed by a battle which was almost entirely fought by galloglas on both sides. At first it looked as if Bourke would be the victor, then at the eleventh hour his force was scattered by Fitton's cavalry which he had kept out of sight to use as a last resort. But it was not a decisive victory and the Bourkes and Clandonnells left the field, dispersed, then headed home for Mayo. It is not clear what part Richard-an-Iarainn played in this, or if he joined his clan chief in battle, but Oliverus Bourke must have been assured of his loyalty, for the following year Richard was officially elected as his tanist. His mother Finola's murderous scheme had finally paid off.

But the involvement of the Bourkes in the rebellion had one very serious result: Sir Henry Sidney finally turned his attention to Mayo in person, noting the fact that neither the Mayo Bourkes nor the O'Malleys had submitted to the Crown. In 1574, as part of the policy of divide and rule, Mayo was divided into ten baronies. The names of the chieftains of the various clans involved are given in official lists, Richard-an-Iarainn being allotted the barony of Burrishoole, his land, according to Knox, consisting of Owle Clan Philbin, Owle Eighter (Iochtarach) and Silocht MacTybbot's land. A year later, in 1575, the Bourkes and the O'Malleys submitted, thus bringing Sidney to Mayo again but without success. Finally, in 1576, he lost all patience and called a meeting of the principal chiefs in Galway, demanding that they attend. In order to ensure Shane Oliverus Bourke's compliance, it is said that he 'lured away' the Clandonnel galloglas so that Bourke could not take his ferocious fighting force with him.

Faced with a no-win situation, Bourke reluctantly complied, bringing with him the lesser chieftains, including the O'Malley. Somewhat to his surprise, as he had been expecting a wild man, Sidney was impressed with Bourke, describing him as 'very sensible' and 'a lover of quiet and civility'. The chief had no English but was able to converse with Sidney in Latin, and the result of his submission was that he would rule by English, not brehon, law, pay two hundred and fifty pounds a year in tax to the Crown and provide Sidney with two hundred soldiers for two months each year. In exchange Bourke was generously given his own lands back on his promise that he would hold them for the Queen and also 'do his best to expel the Scots who swarm in these quarters'.

There is no official mention of Grace in the early 1570s so it is reasonable to assume that she was carrying on with her activities much as usual. As for Tibbot who, according to a sixteenth-century Irish poet in a description worthy of a Mills and Boon novel, had golden ringlets, hawk-like blue eyes, ruddy cheeks and when he reached manhood was loved by all the girls in Ireland, he was safely out of the way of all the political activity and warfare. It was the Irish custom, as it used to be in the days of knights and squires in early mediaeval England, for the son of a chieftain to be sent to the house of another to be 'fostered and educated'. Tibbot, therefore, was handed over to Edmund MacTibbot, a vassal chief of the MacWilliams who lived at Castelleaffy. One of the main reasons for the practice was that it would ensure that from then on the fostered child would always be able to count on the loyalty of the fostering family. In return, the boy's family offered support and protection. In Tibbot's case, it had the added advantage of allowing his mother to get on with her various activities without having to worry about him.

The 'education' given to Tibbot was virtually the same as that given to the children of thirteenth- and fourteenth-century English knights. Of primary importance would be the ability to ride and fight well. He would learn how to fight with sword, dagger and javelin, working on the skills until he became proficient in all. Since Tibbot was also able to read and write in both English and Irish, Edmund MacTibbot must have had a tutor for him, most probably a priest. He was also made familiar with both English and brehon law. By the standards of the day, Tibbot was given an excellent, all-round, education.

But if Grace was still practising piracy, how was it that she was able to get away with it for so long? The obvious explanation is that preventing her activities was simply too difficult. To mount a blockade at sea, say, outside Galway harbour or Clew Bay, or keep English ships standing by somewhere on the Atlantic coast ready to intercept her fleet, would have been extremely expensive, time-consuming and almost certain to fail. Yet there would have been other ways. A determined land force might have taken her at Rockfleet, as was attempted later. Less spectacular but probably more effective was to use other means. She had enough enemies for one of them to have been primed to wait his chance and kill her, particularly if a reward was involved. She could have been enticed into some kind of trap; instead – nothing.

Another possible explanation has been suggested: that either on her own account, or working through an intermediary, she was acting as an 'intelligencer' for the English government: in other words as a spy. Her extensive knowledge of the shipping using the west-coast sea lanes, her 'maintenance' system of stopping all vessels and demanding tolls, would make her enormously useful, especially where the movements of Spanish vessels were concerned. She would know if the pattern of shipping changed and if so, in what way; what kind of ships were being used by the Spaniards and what they were carrying, whether they were armed and, if so, the nature of the armaments.

If this was the case, then it might also explain the ambivalence of Irish historians towards Grace. She might well have been described from time to time by the English as a traitor, but was she also considered a traitor to her own people? On at least two future occasions she would escape hanging by the English when those with her who had committed similar or even lesser transgressions went to the gallows regardless. It would also help explain why so strong a personality, so powerful a seafarer and the wife of a Bourke who would go on to become 'the MacWilliam' is totally missing from contemporary accounts in her own country. What we get in spades is romance: Grace the 'pirate queen', laughing, gambling, swearing and sleeping with her band of pirates, defying everyone, rather than Grace the pragmatist, the woman determined on her own survival, and that of her youngest son, a woman who was prepared to burn, steal, fight and often kill to that end.

Although there is no record of it in State Papers, it is said that sometime during 1574/75 Grace and Richard actually visited London. If so, then for what reason and what did they do there? Was it because people in high places wanted to question Grace? Did she meet up with specific contacts and pass on information? She would have been quite capable of discussing the situation, as we know from her recorded later visit that she was perfectly well able to converse in Latin.

This would seem a good moment to relate one of the great Grace legends, for some accounts say that it was on her way back from this visit to London that the event took place. However, since Richard-an-Iarainn plays no part in it, that seems unlikely unless they were travelling back on separate ships. The tale concerns Howth Castle, the seat of the St Lawrence family on the coast some ten miles out of Dublin. As ever, there are several versions of the story. Morton, quoting Owen Blackburn in *Illustrious Irishwomen*, writes: 'When Grainne was returning to Connaught, a storm came on and she was obliged to put into Howth Harbour. She landed and advancing to the castle found the door shut and the family at dinner. Being refused the hospitality she demanded for herself and her followers, she retraced her steps towards the shore. On her way she met a beautiful child playing in the grounds, and hearing he was the heir to Howth, Grainne deliberately stole him. She bore off her prize with her to Connaught, nor would she give him up until she stipulated for, and obtained as her ransom, the promise that for ever at mealtimes the doors of the castle would be thrown wide open and hospitality extended to all wayfarers who should demand it. This custom is still observed there'.

In another version she put into Howth for food and provisions for her followers, then, as the wife of a chieftain, went to the castle expecting the hospitality extended to one of her rank according to Irish custom. But in Howth, it being within the Pale, Irish customs did not apply and so the gates were locked against her. When she remonstrated and demanded to see Lord Howth, she was told to go away, he was at dinner. She returned in a fury to the beach and there she found Lord Howth's young grandson whom she promptly kidnapped, returning with him to Clew Bay. Lord Howth and his followers set off at once in pursuit, bringing with them a ransom of silver and gold to give to Grace in exchange for the boy, but Grace refused it, instead making him swear a solemn oath that from then on the gates of Howth Castle would remain open and that an extra place would always be set at dinner for any traveller who might need it.

According to Anne Chambers, the event is recorded in the St Lawrence family archive, which states that Lord Howth gave a ring to Grace as a pledge of the agreement and that it was preserved in the O'Malley family until 1795 when an Elizabeth O'Malley married John Irwin of Camlin, county Roscommon, taking the ring with her. After that Irwin's son, a solicitor, emigrated to America taking the ring with him, passing it on in turn to his grandson who had it made into a brooch. Legend or not, true or not, at Howth Castle there is always a spare place set at table.

7

Captured!

In March 1577 Grace, entirely of her own volition, went
to Galway city to meet Lord Deputy Sir Henry Sidney.
Her fame, or rather notoriety, had by now spread
throughout the country. It is from now on that details
of her activities appear in the *Calendars of State Papers*
and from this point in her career that she was of sufficient interest for later historians to include her, however
briefly, in their works. In his account of the rebellion by
the Clannrickards and some of the Bourkes, Knox says
that although Earl Richard of Clannrickard was loyal,
his two sons, Ulrick and John, led resistance to the
President whose orders were to introduce English law
and abolish 'Irish cuttings and spendings'. The 'rising up
of the Bourkes' was 'supported by Grania, Queen of Clare
Island and Clew Bay, a famous commander of war
galleys', and, echoing contemporary English accounts,
'for forty years the stay of all rebellions in the west'.

Sidney put down the Clannrickard rebellion and gave
chase to the rebellious Bourkes without catching up with
them, but he did succeed in forcing the Clandonnell
galloglas over the border into Ulster. For a brief time,
thereafter, Connaught was quiet in the iron grip of its
President, Sir William Malby, with his deserved reputation for putting down any stirrings of revolt with
extreme savagery.

While dealing with the Clannrickards and chasing the
galloglas, Sidney had been accompanied by his famous

son, the poet Philip (later, Sir Philip) Sidney who had come over to Ireland with his close friend, the Earl of Essex. Essex, however, was ill and had been left behind in Dublin Castle. Perhaps a word is needed here on the Elizabethan soldier-poets who did service in Ireland. They come down to us in history as true Renaissance men, many-talented and equally able to fight bravely, charm a lady and adeptly turn out a pretty verse. But Irish history paints a different picture. Setting aside Walter Raleigh, who was primarily a soldier and adventurer, both Philip Sidney and Edmund Spencer fully supported the measures taken to control the 'uncivilised' Irish. Indeed Spencer, he of *The Faerie Queen*, did not think the Lord Deputy or his subordinates were tough enough and wanted even more Draconian measures taken at the very first sign of revolt. 'Troops,' he wrote, 'should tread down all before them and lay on the ground all the stiff-necked people of the land.'

So, when Sir Henry met Grace, accompanied by Richard-an-Iarainn, Philip was there to witness it. The natural order of things would have been for Sidney to negotiate with Richard while his wife stood dutifully on the sidelines, taking no part in the discussion. After all, this was 'Iron Richard', that 'plundering, warlike, unjust and rebellious man' who allegedly hardly ever took off his armour even at home. But Sidney must have got the measure of the relationship straight away. Later, in 1582, when writing his journal, he said:

> There came to mee also a most famous femynyne sea capten called Grany Imallye, and offered her service unto me, wheresoever I woulde command her, with three galleys and two hundred fightinge men, either in Ireland or Scottland. She brought with her her husband, for she was as well by sea as by land well *more than Mrs Mate with him* [my italics]. He was of the

Nether Burkes and now, as I here (sic) Mackwilliam
Euter and called by nickname Richard In Iron. This
was a most notorious woman in all the costes of
Ireland.

'This woman', he was to write to Sir Francis Walsingham
at the time, 'Philip Sidney did see and speak with; he can
more at large inform you of her.' Sadly, we do not know
what she and Sidney discussed although it is said their
conversation was in Latin. Sidney's estimate of Grace has
gone down in history. As Knox puts it: 'he who ruled his
foes, failed to rule his wife at home'.

There is no explanation as to why Grace chose that
particular moment to submit herself to Sidney, though
since she rarely acted on impulse, she must have felt she
had good reason to do so. One suggestion is that it was
to ensure that Richard did eventually become the
MacWilliam by officially and publicly recognising
English rule and offering the use of her fleet, while at
the same time allowing Sidney to see just how powerful
she was. But it left her open to the charges of being
prepared to play both ends against the middle to achieve
her own ends, and of currying favour with the English,
thus betraying her own people. But whatever her reasoning, she proved to have miscalculated the situation and
for the first time was about to run into serious trouble.

For many years the Earl of Desmond, whose vast lands
were in the south of the country, had proved a thorn in
the side of successive English administrations. In part
this was due to the enmity between Desmond (who needs
a book to himself) and the Earl of Ormond. In 1564 they
had quarrelled so fiercely that words turned to blows
and blows to what was described as 'a private battle on
the soil of the British Isles between the two noblemen'.
The Queen was furious at this *lèse majesté* and immediately summoned them both to London, where they were

made to enter into recognisances to keep the peace and thereafter to abide by whatever judgement might be handed down. But the antagonism of the two Earls was soon reflected in London, both men having their enthusiastic supporters among the different factions at the English Court, which was scarcely what had been intended. On this occasion, Sidney actually took Desmond's side and persuaded the Queen to allow him to return to Ireland, while Ormond remained behind in London.

But Desmond was to remain a worry and several attempts were made to keep him in line. In 1571 he signed articles pledging himself to abandon the Irish customs 'of coyne and livery' on his estate and to disband his galloglas (which he certainly did not do). In 1573 he went to Dublin where his behaviour, and refusal to make any further pledges regarding his behaviour, gave rise to sufficient concern for him to be held there, a virtual prisoner. Then in November he escaped, made his way to Munster and, in a poetic phrase, 'took to the fern'. But in actual fact he did nothing for which he could be called to account and a year later surrendered of his own free will. Once more he was sufficiently persuasive to be given the benefit of the doubt and he retired again to his castle at Askeaton.

But his was an unstable character, and although he was for the present behaving himself and doing as he had promised, behind the scenes he was being pulled in several directions at once. While some members of his family thought it politic to keep quiet for the time being and do nothing, he was seen by others as the possible leader of an anti-Protestant, anti-English party backed by Spain and the Pope. Not to mention that on the English side there were those who, observing his great estates and wealth, were looking at ways of getting some of it for themselves and were prepared to act as *agents provocateurs* to bring this about. So by 1577, although Desmond was, apparently, behaving himself, nobody trusted him and he was coming under increasing suspicion in London as a fomenter of Catholic plots against the Queen.

However, while Desmond was carefully avoiding anything that might arouse English hostility, it occurred to him that it would be useful if he could come up with something that would apparently prove his loyalty to the Queen beyond doubt. Which was when Grace played right into his hands.

She must have convinced herself that her 'submission' to the Lord Deputy had put everything right between her and the English administration and that there was nothing to prevent her carrying on as usual. It proved to be a major miscalculation. Only weeks after the meeting in Galway, she sailed south down the coast to Desmond country, bent on plunder. She would have been well aware of the ambivalent attitude of the English government to Desmond and presumably thought she could get away with it. So it was that for the first time her luck ran out.

She was caught by Desmond's men and taken to the Earl at Askeaton Castle. He saw at once how this might benefit him. Now he had, under his roof and as his prisoner, the notorious pirate who had played havoc for years with ships going about their lawful business around the coasts of Ireland. Determined to make the most of his prize, he ensured that she was incarcerated in Limerick Gaol straight away with no way of escape. For a free spirit like Grace, who had never previously been confined in any way, imprisonment must have come hard indeed. As to Richard-an-Iarainn's reaction, there is nothing that suggests he made any effort to secure his wife's freedom.

In March 1578, after Grace had already been a prisoner for many months, the new President of Munster, Lord Justice Drury, visited the Earl in his castle in search of further verification of Desmond's continuing loyalty. Desmond had the very thing: the pirate queen, Grace O'Malley, and he duly produced her from prison as proof of his loyalty to the Crown.

Drury was suitably impressed and immediately wrote to Sidney in Dublin informing him that Desmond was holding an exceptionally important and dangerous prisoner: 'Granye O'Mayle, a woman that hath impudently passed the part of womanhood and been a great spoiler, and chief commander and director of thieves and murderers at sea to spoil this province'. It would be interesting to know what Sidney made of it, so soon after 'Mrs Mate', the lady who wore the breeches, had submitted herself to English rule, but there is no record of his reply or reference to it in his *Narratives*.

Gleefully, Drury also wrote to Sir Francis Walsingham telling him how Desmond 'sent in also unto me, Granny Nye Male, one of power and forces'. Walsingham duly informed the Privy Council and Desmond's action appears to have convinced them that at the present time the Earl posed no threat. In a letter to Drury Walsingham wrote: 'We pray you also to signify to the Earl of Desmond in whose good part her Majesty and we take it to understand of his so good and dutiful behaviour, in making such a demonstration of his loyalty, as you write of, not only in words but also in sending unto you Grany O'Mayle and other notorious offenders of his country'.

Drury was taking no chances. He decided his star prisoner should be moved from Limerick and secured in Dublin Castle. So, eighteen months after her original capture she was taken, securely shackled, to Dublin. So concerned was Drury that nothing should go amiss that he met up with the troop escorting her at Leighlin in County Carlow and himself rode with the party to Dublin.

Once he had her safely under lock and key he informed the Privy Council:

To that place was brought unto me Granie ny Maille,
a woman of the province of Connaught, governing
a country of the O'Flaherties [which suggests he had
not caught up with the fact that Grace had married
again], famous for her stoutness of courage and
person and for some sundry exploits at sea. She was
taken by the Earl of Desmond a year and a half ago
and hath remained partly with him and partly in
her Majesty's gaol of Limerick and was sent now to
come to Dublin where she is remaining.

Interestingly, this does suggest that Grace had not spent
all her time in Limerick Gaol but that from time to time,
for some periods, she was imprisoned at Askeaton.

Imprisonment in Dublin Castle was the Irish equiva-
lent of imprisonment in the Tower of London. From the
'status' point of view where gaols were concerned, on a
scale of one to ten Dublin Castle was ten. It meant that
you were politically important and dangerous. Also, as
with its London counterpart, more often your 'release'
meant only that you were free to leave your cell to ascend
the steps of a scaffold, a fate which befell many of her
fellow-prisoners while Grace was incarcerated there.

Then, for no apparent reason, very early in 1579 she
was suddenly released without charge. Could it be that
having involuntarily assisted Desmond in proving his
loyalty to the Crown, she had served her purpose and
might prove far more useful returning to her usual activities which would enable her to provide the government
with desperately needed information on the patterns of
Spanish shipping?

But her release from Dublin was not without incident.
As soon as was practicable she returned to Rockfleet
Castle. It is difficult to know whether what happened
subsequently was on orders from Dublin or London to
make sure she was kept in her place, or was more of a

freelance venture. Either way, on 8 March she found herself under siege by land and sea from a force headed by Captain William Martin. The pretext for this was that he had been begged to do so by the merchants of Galway city, now faced once again with the prospect of their shipping being regularly interfered with en route for the port. However, after eighteen days Grace triumphed. One account suggests that Martin was called off by a higher authority, but the popular view is that she put up such a stout defence that she drove Martin's land and sea forces away and that he narrowly escaped being taken prisoner. If she was able to muster her galleys to cut off Martin's escape by sea and hem in his ship or ships, then it would have been relatively easy for the Bourkes and their galloglas to cut them off by road, so this might well have been the case. Whatever the truth, by the summer Grace had returned to practising maintenance by sea and land.

The possibility that she was released from Dublin Castle in exchange for providing intelligence certainly makes sense, given what was to happen next. For it was then that the Desmond family chose to corroborate all Elizabeth's worst fears and provide her government with cast-iron proof, if it were needed, that Spain was prepared to use Ireland as a stepping stone for an assault on England.

In 1569 a man who is described as 'a clever, flashy and disreputable adventurer, an English and a Catholic with piracy in his past', arrived in Spain from Ireland and for some time lived there in luxury at the expense of the Spanish government. Thomas Stukeley, like both of Grace's husbands, enjoyed fighting more than anything else and in repayment for Spanish hospitality is said to have taken part in the Battle of Lepanto. Meanwhile the Earl of Desmond's cousin, James Fitzmaurice, after spending two years in France, had gone to Rome to ask for help to invade Ireland. Here he met up with Stukeley who had exactly the same aim in mind. So, having taken soundings and with reasonable expectations of success, the two men started raising an army of mercenaries, but both the Pope and Philip II were loathe to risk their own men and so the invasion force was largely made up of felons, robbers and 'highwaymen skulking in the Apennines', induced to enlist in return for a pardon, along with some dissident Irish and Englishmen.

Fitzmaurice also had a promise from Spain of ships for his force. By the time he reached Cadiz with his ragtaggle army the Pope had bestowed upon him the titles of 'Marquess of Leinster' and 'General of our Most Holy Father Gregory XIII, Pontifico Maximo'. He and Stukeley then went on with their ships to Lisbon where Stukeley, for no good reason, except his love of warfare, and with disastrous results, was sidetracked into fighting for the King of Portugal in Morocco in a battle in which the King was killed.

Nothing daunted, Fitzmaurice, although he had lost half his force, pressed on with his invasion of Ireland. At which point the intelligence finally reached Sir William Drury who passed it on at once to the Queen and Privy Council. On 17 July 1579 Fitzmaurice sailed into Dingle Bay with a force varying, depending on which source one believes, from one to six hundred men: Spaniards, French, Italians and a handful of Irish and English. In charge of what we might now call his public relations was a Jesuit priest, Dr Nicholas Sanders, notorious for his attacks on the Queen. Printed proclamations announced in both English and Latin that the Pope had dispossessed Queen Elizabeth of her unjust possession of her kingdom and appointed Fitzmaurice his captain. He was fighting against an unlawful monarch, 'against a tyrant who refuseth to hear Christ speaking by his Vicar'.

There were only just over a thousand English troops in the country and panic set in as the Privy Council

ordered the conscription of every able-bodied man in the
Pale, while also sending recruiting officers down to
Devon and Cornwall to either conscript or impress men.
It was known that the Earl of Desmond had very little
time for his kinsmen and it looked at this stage as if he
did intend to remain loyal. Drury therefore sent Sir
Henry Davells to him at Askeaton, pleading with him
for sixty musketeers and his entire force of galloglas, the
very same galloglas the Earl was supposed to have
disbanded. Desmond, always a ditherer and now under
great pressure from various kinsmen, could not decide
what to do. In the event his mind was made up for him,
for that same night Davells and his companion, Arthur
Carter, Provost of Munster, were murdered in their beds
while sleeping at a local inn. The murder was carried out
by another member of the Desmond family on the orders
of Fitzmaurice who saw it as a way to force the Earl on
to his side. That done, he set out for Connaught.

Desmond planned to go into Connaught through
Ulster, knowing that Tirlagh O'Neill was sympathetic,
had thousands of fighting men at the ready and might
well be prepared to join forces. But to do so he had to
cross Bourke land, where he 'commandeered' horses and
provender, which enraged the local population and the
Bourkes' galloglas. As a result, a troop of galloglas chased
after him and shot him dead. The country was about to
go up in flames and all eyes turned to the Earl. It did not
help that a force under Sir Nicholas Malby promptly
marched on Askeaton Castle, looting, burning and
killing as it went even though, as Desmond rightly
pointed out, he had not as yet given his support to
Fitzmaurice but that in spite of this Malby had 'wantonly'
attacked his men. Even at this eleventh hour, however,
the English administration hoped for peace. Desmond's
old enemy, the Earl of Ormonde, visited him to urge him
to give up all thought of leading a rebellion which could

only lead to a bloodbath, for however much Ormonde might dislike Desmond, he truly wanted to do everything possible to avoid a major war on Irish soil.

Again Desmond hesitated, this time for so long that the Spanish Ambassador told Philip II that he had gone over to the Queen. Eventually English patience ran out. Desmond was given until 8 a.m. on 2 November to give himself up to the Lord Justice who would then accompany him to England to state his case. Desmond never arrived and he was at once proclaimed a traitor, accused of conniving with foreign powers to allow troops into Ireland using his cousin, Fitzmaurice; of the murders of Davells and Carter; and of sending his galloglas to fight on Fitzmaurice's side. The die was cast and the consequent conflagration would last four years.

Desmond immediately asked the Macwilliam and Richard-an-Iarainn to raise Mayo in his cause. The Macwilliam refused. He had made his submission after much thought and intended to stand by it. Whether or not it was because at that time Richard's hopes of becoming the Macwilliam seemed as remote as ever, or whether he really thought he would be on the winning side at the end of the conflict, he agreed to Desmond's plea and with his own men, the Macdonnell galloglas, and a number of O'Flaherties and O'Malleys, took the opportunity to march on the territories of the O'Kellys and Lord Athenry, plundering and looting as he went. One suggestion is that Richard behaved as he did simply because the Macwilliam, whose position he so coveted, was on the other side. It was not an intelligent decision but then, whatever Richard might have been renowned for, it was not the strength of his intellect.

So what about Grace? Although she has passed into history as the fomenter of all rebellions, there is no proof that she had a hand in this one, not least because she was unlikely to want to put the lives of herself and her son at risk for the sake of the man who had kept her in prison for the best part of two years. She therefore stayed exactly where she was, at Rockfleet. Subsequent events appear to bear out the fact that during the ensuing months she kept well out of it.

8

Grace of the Gamblers

By now Grace was in her mid to late forties, well past what was considered the prime of life for a woman, but what is remarkable is that never, over all the years she was involved in piracy and even well into her sixties, was there a single known instance of the men she led turning against her or losing faith in her. Their mothers and grandmothers might by now be sitting in the chimney corner telling their beads and waiting for the Grim Reaper to call them to final Judgement, but Grace was as active as ever. To have lived as long as she did, she must have been blessed with excellent health, coupled with plenty of energy, for while Richard-an-Iarainn was busy plotting and rebelling she never for a moment let up on her own activities, whether personally leading her men on land raids on property or harrying ships in the sea lanes. The nickname 'Grace of the Gamblers' or 'Gamesters' referred both to her own passion for dice and cards but also to her predilection for surrounding herself with like-minded souls as prepared as she was to take risks whenever she demanded it of them.

Nor did her loyalties elsewhere make any difference though it would be interesting to know what her men made of them, not only politically but also, if her reputation is deserved, of her taking a lover whenever a suitable candidate took her fancy. The reasoning behind the marriages, however, would be well understood, each husband giving her official married status and tying her through her children into two major clans, although it must have been a matter for joking comment that neither 'Donal of the Battles' nor 'Iron Richard' ever managed to get the better of Grace O'Malley. As a mother, too, she had done the best for her children. Of the children of the O'Flaherty marriage, two of them, no doubt at Grace's instigation, had been firmly stitched into the fabric of the Bourke clan: the eldest son, Owen, was married to the daughter of Edmund Bourke of Castlebar, while her daughter, Margaret, was now the wife of yet another Richard Bourke, later to become known as 'the Devil's Hook', a sobriquet occasionally attached to Grace. Tibbot, meanwhile, was being brought up as befitted the son of a clan chief but it was clear that he was also being groomed to follow in his mother's footsteps when she finally gave up seafaring, and presumably this was accepted. But what is virtually unique in the history of the times is that the loyalty of her men would remain unaffected by the internecine clan quarrels, inter-clan wars and all the blood-drenched turmoil of sixteenth-century Ireland.

In 1578 Sidney was recalled from his post as Lord Deputy of Ireland and returned to England and Ludlow, resuming a position he had held earlier in his career, that of President of the Welsh Council. The reasons for the recall are confused but certainly have to do with what was seen in London as a rapidly deteriorating situation in Munster. There were also what are described as 'a cloud of allegations' to the effect that he had feathered his own nest and 'taken land to farm'.

Five years later, in an attempt to tell his side of the story, he embarked on his *Narratives*: a brief résumé (laced with hindsight) of his time as Lord Deputy. There were three drafts, all intended for Sir Francis Walsingham who, as well as being Secretary of State to the Privy Council and thus a person of great influence, was also about to be linked to Sidney by more personal ties as his daughter was affianced to Philip Sidney. There are two clear messages that come through the *Narratives*: firstly, Sidney's belief that he should have received some kind of compensation for ever having taken on 'this thankless task'. In a letter from Ludlow Castle on 1 May 1582, written 'with more pain than I can bear', he speaks of his neglect by the government in spite of his services to her Majesty, describing himself at fifty-four years of age as now 'toothless, trembling and being £5000 in debt'. If he had not succeeded in pacifying the country, it was not for want of trying 'or lack of summary measures', indeed he boasts that once, to make a point and as an example to others, 'I hanged a Scots captain and near twenty of his men'.

Secondly, he was convinced to the point of paranoia that he was beset by enemies on all sides, but by one in particular. This was Thomas Butler, 10th Earl of Ormond, a relation of the Boleyns who was consistently loyal to the Crown and consequently well thought of in London. Sidney believed his was a malign influence at Court and that Ormond was constantly, as we would say now, briefing against him. Sidney blamed him for just about every setback he had experienced during both tours of duty in Ireland. There was also a cast of lesser villains, including Shane O'Neill, the Earls of Clanrickard and Essex, and the Lord Chancellor, Sir William Gerrard. While it is too simplistic to say that his view was that everyone was out of step except Sidney, the *Narratives* do give a chilling, if confusing, picture of the politics and intrigues of the Irish wars. As to his desire for compensation in the way of lands, titles and other royal favours, the Queen remained adamant that he had been compensated enough. Sidney's bitterness stayed with him to the end of his life.

After Sidney's recall a considerable time was to pass before the Queen appointed a successor. However, Sir William Pelham, an acknowledged expert on fortifications, became to all intents and purposes the acting Lord Deputy of Ireland, and to him fell the task of dealing with the continuing Desmond rebellion and bringing the Earl himself to justice. The matter was one of increasing urgency for the Queen, not only because of the threat of political unrest and foreign invasion, but because the wars in Ireland were proving extremely expensive. She was even said to have had her doubts about officially proclaiming Desmond a traitor, not because she did not think he was, or felt any sympathy for him, but because of the expense of any campaign launched against him.

When such a campaign was finally agreed, the early preparations for it were chaotic, in no small part because of the likely cost and the consequent penny-pinching that went on, but at last everything was as ready as it was likely to be and in February 1580 Pelham, at the head of about a thousand men, on horse and foot, set out for Waterford en route for Limerick and the Desmond lands in the south. The campaign was to last for months. From the outset precious little mercy was shown to those who stood in Pelham's way, although it should be pointed out that he was only continuing the policy of his predecessors. His troops burned and razed their way through the countryside, laying it waste and stealing anything and everything they could. But the 'carrying away of cattle and other property to the Lord Justice's camp' was only the half of it. The unfortunate people who got in their way fared even worse. As the *Annals of the Four Masters* describe it: 'It was not wonderful that they should kill men fit for action, but they killed also blind and feeble men, women, boys and girls, sick persons, idiots and old people'.

Meanwhile Richard-an Iarainn was taking full advantage of the fact that the English military effort was concentrated in the south. His forays were growing ever more daring until he was raiding land and property down as far as Galway city. It could not be allowed to continue and Sir Nicholas Malby was, therefore, sent back up to Connaught to settle the matter once and for all. He was joined in campaign by a new and powerful ally, the MacWilliam, Shane Oliverus, who remained loyal to the Crown not least because he had now officially bypassed Richard-an-Iarainn's elected claim to his title on his death in favour of his own brother, a move which had been agreed and recognised by the English administration, which would be the case under the English system.

Malby and the Macwilliam, accompanied by a substantial number of their own men and a large force of Scots, marched on Galway and together succeeded in driving Richard-an Iarainn out of the area and back into Mayo, by which time his own galloglas had seen the writing on the wall and were deserting him in droves. Malby then continued on to one of Richard's strongholds, Donamona Castle, where, as he reported to London, 'I put the band (i.e. the garrison of the castle), men, women and children to the sword, whereupon all the other castles in the area were given up without resistance'. In blind panic, Richard and his remaining followers fled from the mainland of Mayo and holed up on an island in Clew Bay. One account also claims that Malby then commandeered 'all the boats' and that during 'the maritime campaign' which followed over a hundred Bourke followers died of starvation. It does not say, however, whether any of the boats involved belonged to Grace. Given the circumstances, it seems likely that Grace had ensured her own vessels were elsewhere.

In a report back to the Lord Deputy, Malby informs him that he has removed to Burrishoole 'upon a riverside where a ship of five hundred tons might be at anchor

1. Rockfleet Castle

2. Irish warriors and peasants, by Albrecht Dürer, 1521

3. Triumphant return of English soldiers. From Derricke's *Images of Ireland*, 1581.

4. A Gaelic chieftain. Derricke, 1581.

5. The MacSweeney chieftain feasting out-of-doors. Derricke, 1581.

6. Grace O' Malley's castle on Clare Island.

at low water'. Nearby there was a plentiful iron mine as well as good arable land and pasture. Out in Clew Bay, he wrote, 'lieth many fair islands . . . and there cometh every year about fifty English ships for the fishing. They have been before this time compelled to pay a great tribute to the O'Malleys, which I have forbidden until her Majesty's pleasure be known. It is accounted one of the best fishing places in Ireland for salmon, herring and all kinds of sea fish'.

As to his quarry, Richard-an-Iarainn, 'he, considering that the Clandonnels galloglas forsook him and that he was narrowly prosecuted by me and my companions in all parts of the country, not being able to keep the field nor to make any resist (sic), fled to the islands with some Scots and some gentlemen of his own retinue'.

It was beginning to look as if Malby was settling in at Burrishoole for the duration, a possibility which must have alarmed Grace, for it was then that she took a hand in affairs. 'On the 16th I removed to Ballyknock,' writes Malby, 'whither Grainne O'Malley and certain of her kinsmen came to me.' It is clear, therefore, that her reputation was such that even though she was officially merely the wife of his antagonist, he was prepared to negotiate directly with her in her own right. However, since he had stationed a substantial garrison right next to Burrishoole Abbey, in the heart of O'Malley territory, she must have known she had little alternative but to treat with him if she did not want to lose everything. What mattered now was to get the best deal possible. Unless they leave written accounts of what motivated them at the time, one hesitates to attribute emotions to historical characters, but the onlooker is left feeling that by this time Grace must have become heartily sick of extricating Richard from his self-inflicted troubles.

Richard, on the other hand, was still trying to negotiate for himself from his increasingly weak position on his island but eventually, after Grace's intervention, he was persuaded to return to the mainland to make yet another formal submission. Then, having at last come to an agreement, he was genuinely delayed out in the middle of Clew Bay by almost a week of bad weather. It was at this point that Pelham, still struggling to quell the Desmond rebellion in Munster, sent for Malby to join him with his forces as soon as possible and Malby had no alternative but to do as he was told. So far as Pelham was concerned, Malby had succeeded in his task of putting down the Bourke revolt in Mayo and there was no reason for him to stay any longer. Pelham's reason for taking this decision when he did is explained in the *Calendars of State Papers*: Sir Nicholas Malby had been recalled south 'as he has put an end to the stirs in Connaught by Richard Ineran, husband of Grany O'Maille'. Malby was loathe to leave behind such unfinished business and had no intention of letting Richard off the hook, and before he left he ordered that Richard's official submission be sent on to him in Munster for his approval.

There is a strong suggestion that Grace then told her husband how to play it if they did not want to bring down even more trouble on their heads. His submission was to be suitably contrite. In it he freely admitted that he had fallen away from his duty towards God and Her Majesty and promised that he would now make amends. However, still with an eye to the main chance he would, he said, call back his followers if Her Majesty so wished in order that they could return to their homes and lands with their property. This would mean that Her Majesty would not lose the rents and duties owed to her. Also, although he did not so phrase it – and again one suspects the hand of Grace – he hinted that with Malby gone there was now a noticeable power vacuum in Mayo. Therefore he pleaded for the restoration of his right at least to be chief of the Lower Bourkes and once again take up such duties and demands as from time to time became due from him and his followers. Whatever reservations he might have had about it – and one imagines he had a few – Malby, unable to leave Munster, had to agree and Richard duly signed his submission with his mark.

Then, just as it was beginning to look as if Pelham might actually succeed in pacifying the south and the country was quietening down, the Queen finally appointed a new Lord Deputy: Arthur, Lord Grey de Wilton. The appointment came at the worst possible time, just as Desmond was finally beginning to talk seriously of surrender. His wife, Lady Desmond, had actually come in person to discuss possible terms with Pelham, while the Earl himself was approaching the English Admiral, Sir William Winter, to ask for a passage to England in a last attempt to secure some kind of pardon. Now everything was thrown into confusion again.

The Council had hoped that Pelham, although he might rightly have expected to be officially appointed Lord Deputy himself, would remain in Ireland and continue his service under Grey. But he patently did not wish to do so and, pleading ill health, he returned to England. Writing of the decision to appoint Grey to the post, Cyril Falls says: 'It was a tragedy, not least from the point of view of the Geraldines (i.e. the Desmonds and their followers) themselves, that the change should have come at such a moment, since the horrors that followed might have been avoided had Pelham been able to pursue his policy only a little longer'. 'Wilton,' he continues, 'showed great energy in Ireland, but it was not always well directed': an enormous understatement. Among the staff Grey brought with him were Edmund Spenser as his secretary and Walter Raleigh as one of his captains.

Almost immediately there followed an event which

might well have come under the heading of black comedy had its end not been so appalling and its consequences so serious. Admiral Sir William Winter had been pleading with Pelham to allow him to return to England to restock his ships and for essential repairs but Pelham had consistently refused to give his permission. However, in September, with a new Lord Deputy in place, he took advantage of the new appointment and sailed for England. Intelligence-gathering must have been poor, for he had no reason to expect trouble.

But six days later, totally out of the blue there was another foreign invasion of Ireland, this time by a force allegedly raised by the Pope himself. From the first it was a forlorn venture and never for a moment posed any real threat. The force was made up almost entirely of Italians, although much of the funding was said to have been provided by King Philip of Spain. The foreigners landed at Smerwick which is almost on the end of the Dingle peninsula. Grey was in Dublin, but even so it seems almost unbelievable that it took three weeks for rumours of the landing to reach him. When they did, he promptly dismissed them, informing the Queen that he did not believe them.

The Earl of Ormonde, however, did, and with a small band of his own men went to see for himself. The foreigners had commandeered the nearby fort of Dun an Oir, which had been used earlier by Fitzmaurice, and they were busy strengthening it. Ormond managed to capture several of the foreigners and from them learned that their entire force consisted of under seven hundred men, although they had brought with them extra supplies in the expectation of reinforcements. Ormond saw the invasion force as something which could easily be dealt with, and having sent confirmation to Grey that the landing had really happened, he returned to harrying the rebels in the north while keeping an eye on his own estates.

Finally convinced, Grey rode out of Dublin at the head
of eight hundred troops bound for the Dingle peninsula
where he encamped while awaiting the return of Winter
with ships mounted with heavy guns suitable for a
bombardment, as well as provisions. By early November
the scene was set for one of the very worst episodes in
the history of the Irish wars. Grey besieged the intruders'
fort on land, while Winter's ships blockaded them from
the sea. For several days the Italians held out until they
were overcome by the superior firepower of Winter's
naval guns. Within hours a man appeared holding a
white sheet and asking for a parley. This was agreed and
the commander of the camp, Bastiano di San Guiseppi,
came in person, along with several others, to beg that his
garrison be allowed to depart at once and in peace. Grey
asked if there were any Spaniards present, for if there
were he must talk with them. A Spanish captain joined
the other envoys. Had the force been sent to Ireland by
Philip of Spain, demanded Grey.

He was told that they had not. It was claimed in reports
sent back to London that the Spanish captain and the
commander then told Grey that the invasion force had
been sent on the orders of the Pope 'for the defence of
the Catholic faith'. Deeply suspicious, Grey told them that
he would not have been 'astonished' if subjects of the
Philip II *had* become involved in such an enterprise and
that their fault was aggravated by 'the vileness of their
commander'.

Yet again, as is so often the case in the Irish wars,
reports differ widely as to exactly what was said, or promised, by Grey, depending on which account you read. Grey
declared afterwards that he told the invaders that he
would not treat with them and that the only conditions
acceptable to him were that they should surrender the
fort, and themselves, 'to his will for life or death'. His
word is supported in part by Edmund Spenser (who could

hardly do anything else since he was Grey's secretary), although his version of what the envoy said to Grey differs substantially. According to Spencer, the envoy told Grey that they had not been hired either by the Pope or Philip of Spain but were simply mercenaries who had come to Ireland to fight for the Irish.

In any event, the outcome was the same. On the morning of 11 November the commander and a dozen officers emerged from the fort, bringing with them their colours. Grey then ordered that all armour and weapons be brought out and laid down on the ground outside and this was duly done, after which the invaders were herded back into the fort. 'Then,' reported Gray, 'put I in certain bands, who straight fell to execution. There were six hundred slain.' Among those 'put in' to see to the slaughter was Captain Walter Raleigh.

'Many more terrible acts,' writes Cyril Falls, 'have been committed in war, but the cold horror of this has continued to leave its mark on the pages of history after over three centuries and a half.' The massacre was greeted with appalled revulsion throughout Ireland, and to this day there is a strong tradition among Irish commentators that Grey promised the garrison mercy if it gave up its arms unconditionally, then reneged on his word. The Queen made no official comment on the event but, according to *The Calendars of State Papers*, wished a few of their officers had been sent to her so that they 'might have had extended to them either justice or mercy'.

One result was that it took the heart out of the Desmond rebels and hastened the end of the revolt. There were repercussions both national and international, but while the Queen never disowned Grey's action, in May 1581 a general pardon was extended to all but a handful of the rebels and in 1582 Wilton was removed from office. His action had proved more even than those within the Pale could stomach, while the Irish regarded him as 'a bloody man who regarded not the life of subjects more than dogs'. But it was not only Smerwick which contributed to his downfall. He had embraced with enthusiasm the old policy of burning crops, 'spoiling the harvest and driving out cattle', taking it to extreme lengths. Even before Grey's arrival Pelham was expressing his strong reservations as to its real cost, reporting that 'the poor people that live only upon labour and fed by their milch cows, offer themselves with their wives and children to be slain by the army rather than suffer the famine that now in extremity is beginning to pinch them'.

Writing some time after the massacre in his *View of the Present State of Ireland*, Edmund Spenser described how 'out of every corner of the woods and glens they came, creeping forth upon their hands, for their legs would not bear them; they looked like anatomies of death, spake like ghosts crying out of their graves . . . yet surely in all this war there perished not so many by the sword, but by the extremity of famine'.

The Smerwick massacre, the scorched-earth policy and near-famine did not, of course, bring about the swift pacification of Ireland, rather the reverse. Then, as in similar situations today, lessons remained unlearned: notably that extreme cruelty and repression breed extreme cruelty and violence in return, violence not least among those who feel they have little or nothing to lose. It also explains why Grace, who had hitherto refrained from overtly supporting the various revolts, was to change her stance during the ensuing years.

With the English forces fully engaged in Munster, first with the invasion and then with mopping up the remnants of the Desmond rebellion, Richard-an-Iarainn, in spite of his official submission, seized the opportunity to confront Malby once again, for in November Shane

Oliverus, 'the MacWilliam', had died suddenly. His title was immediately claimed, as Oliverus had wished, by his brother (also, confusingly, called Richard), citing that it was his right under English law, but Richard and Grace would have none of it and were determined to enforce Richard's claim to the title. During the winter of 1580/81, between them they had an army of '1,200 galloglas, 700 Scots, 300 kerne and 200 horsemen'. As the properly elected tanist to the chieftainship, Richard-an-Iarainn's claim was backed by all the Mayo clan chiefs and the sons of the Earl of Clanrickard. Emboldened by so much support, Richard declared that if he was prevented from succeeding to the chieftainship by peaceful means, as was his due, then he would claim it by force.

News of Richard's stance reached Malby and brought him hotfoot once again to Mayo, but this time he was prepared to talk terms from the outset. Malby was a realist and knew that in view of the recent events in the south there was no possibility that the Queen would agree to the funding of another costly campaign further north. So once again Grace's husband set his mark to a document, this time Letters Patent from the Queen, together with articles of indenture. Lord Grey's signature was also attached.

He is addressed as 'Richard Bourke, alias Richard Inyeren Bourke, alias MacWilliam Eoghter Bourke' who from that date will be the chief of his clan and 'seneschal of the feudal tenants and followers of our people and nation and of his own clan's, and of his own and their lands and tenements'. The point is made that he had acquired the title of the MacWilliam without the Queen's permission but that he had promised to pay in tax each year at Michaelmas term fifty cattle or 250 marks in legal English currency. He also pledged to provide food and lodging for up to two hundred soldiers for forty-two days annually.

Of more concern was the stipulation that he 'would no longer suffer the Scots or other rebels or enemies of her Majesty within the limits of his authority and government'. This was certainly a blow to Grace who had always had her own loyal troop of galloglas. However, to show willing Richard, no doubt lent on heavily by Malby, drove out of Mayo the thousand or so galloglas who had been prepared to fight for him over his claim to the chieftainship.

So far as the Irish were concerned, Richard and Grace had achieved a significant victory. The English government, by the Queen's Letters Patent, had been forced to accept the fact that Richard should succeed to a title conferred on him under the old Irish system, even though for the last fifty years every effort had been made to discontinue the practice. Shortly afterwards, therefore, he was duly elected as the MacWilliam at the Rath of Rausakeera, the ancient meeting place of the Mayo clans, as was the centuries-old tradition. The chieftainship added greatly to his estates, for the title brought with it the castles of Lough Mask and Ballinrobe, along with thousands of acres of land and other properties. There was no knowing what the future might hold, but for the moment both Richard and Grace were satisfied.

9

'. . . She Thinks Herself No Small Lady . . .'

Whatever deal Richard had struck with the English administration in order to save his own skin (even if he had other plans in mind), there was now no possibility of his going back to the old ways without courting danger. Connaught in general and Mayo in particular were no longer part of a western fringe to be left more or less to their own devices, but were very definitely part of the English government's policy for the whole of Ireland. Conquest and the putting down of rebellions were only a part of it; the English administration had many other ways of extending its influence. Among these were settlement and plantation. Families with only the slimmest claims to land through ancient Anglo-Norman ancestry were encouraged to send their sons, particularly their indigent younger sons, over to Ireland to claim their supposed rights; in other words, to colonise the island. Settlement or plantation land was also handed over to those like Edmund Spenser who had, in various capacities, served the Crown in Ireland.

In September 1581 Richard-an-Iarainn received (literally) the ultimate accolade. He was knighted, presumably by the Lord Deputy Grey, on behalf of the Queen, no doubt with the intention of making him part of the very system against which he had rebelled and ensuring that he stuck to the terms of his agreement and kept the peace. But Richard being Richard, within a year he was fighting again. His enemy was his old rival, Richard

MacOliverus, the brother of the previous Macwilliam who was still smarting over the loss of the chieftainship. To rub it in, Richard-an-Iariann raided his namesake's land, claiming that he was doing so in order to collect various rents due to the Crown. In the ensuing battle a number of Richard MacOliverus' clansmen, including his own son, were killed. The incursion rapidly brought down on the raider's head the wrath of Malby who demanded, in view of what he had done, that he hand over one or other of his two elder sons to be held hostage to their father's better behaviour.

Presumably Richard again fell into line for in September 1582 he and Grace were invited by Malby to a meeting and major social event at the governor's own house in Galway. It was a prestigious party to which the Earl of Thomond, Lord Byrmingham, Sir Murrough ne Doe O'Flaherty (he of the recent rebellion) and a whole string of clan chiefs were invited; also their wives. Grace, in her new role of Lady Bourke, succeeded in putting herself forward in a way that led to one of history's most quoted references to her. Malby, duly reporting back to Sir Francis Walsingham on the success of the function, details who attended, pointing out that on this occasion the wives of those involved were also invited and that 'among them Grany O'Mally is one who thinketh herself no small lady'. He concludes by hoping that this new-found amity will lead to peace in the province.

However, today's phrase for what happened next is 'dream on'. Malby had appointed Theobald Dillon as the collector of rents in Connaught but Dillon had ambitions of his own and by some kind of sleight of hand had managed to acquire from the MacCostellos the ownership of the barony of Costello in Mayo by the exploitation of both the English and Irish legal systems. This had made him deeply unpopular. Dillon arrived at Lough Mask Castle, now Richard-an-Iarainn's principal home, and duly demanded from him the sum of £600, claiming this was for rent due under the recent agreement and which was now in arrears.

The response of Richard and Grace was that this was not the case, that the rent had not yet been paid because they were prepared to deal only with the governor, not his agent. What happened next is recorded in *State Papers.* In a letter to Walsingham from Dublin, dated 27 January 1583, Dillon informs him that he has been conscientiously maintaining the law and conferring with the Irish with regard to collecting their rents. However:

> I went their hence to Teyrawle, the farthest part northwarde of MacCalums countrie and told them aforesaid, who dyde swear that they wold in like sort and paid C [one hundred] markes due upon them these five years paste. I then went hence towards the plas where McWilliam was, who met me with his wiyfe, Gran Ne Male, with all their force and did swer they would have my lyfe for coming so fare into their contrie, *and specially his wiyf would fight with me before she was half a mile near me* [my italics].

What followed was obviously a stand-off although Dillon brags that 'I being but a hundred and fifty-four men and fifty horsemen, they was content to yield tho' they were afar greater in number and gave me for my vitalz xxx [thirty] beavys of wine and other provision'.

But Richard obviously had the last word and did indeed deal directly with Malby, for Dillon adds: 'But MacWilliam still came to Sir Nicholas to agree with hym for 600 of areradges [arrears of rent] due upon their contrie, which they never thought to pay'. What Dillon's report reveals is that 'Iron Richard' presumably did not consider he posed a sufficient threat to the rent collector on his own and so threatened him with something far, far worse: the wrath of his terrifying wife who was quite prepared to fight Dillon in person.

One of the major sources regarding Grace then states categorically, twice, that Richard-an-Iarainn died on 30 April 1583. But this could not possibly be, for the problems over the collecting of rents and sorting out who should pay what was finally set down some two years later in a major document entitled *The Composition of Connaught* in which he plays a prominent role and is addressed by various titles which identify him beyond any possibility of mistake.

On the whole the country was quietening down considerably after the Desmond rebellion finally ended in 1583. The writing had been on the wall for over a year for earlier, in January 1582, Sir John Fitzgerald Desmond, on whom the Earl relied heavily, had been ambushed and killed and, as was the barbaric way of the times, his 'turquoise set with gold' was sent to the Queen, his '*agnus dei*' to the Earl of Bedford and his head as 'a New Year present' to Lord Deputy Grey.

By the autumn of 1583 all possible escape routes for Desmond had been blocked and he was on the run accompanied by a only a small body of men. He was also suffering badly from the effects of a wound he had received in a skirmish earlier. Faced with the oncoming winter, he made for one of his old refuges, a wood in Glenageenty below the hill of Slieve Logher. The rebels were running short of food and the next day, November 9, Desmond sent a raiding party out to the lands of a nearby, minor chieftain, Maurice O'Moriarty. Desmond's men would brook no opposition and wounded the chieftain, stripped his wife and children naked and threw them out into the cold, then rounded up their cattle and horses and set off back to Desmond.

After sending word of the raid to the English commander in Dingle, Maurice's brother Owen, infuriated and humiliated at the treatment his family had received, set out with twenty-five of his men, and six soldiers from the garrison at Castlemaine, bent on revenge. They successfully tracked the cattle to where Desmond was hiding out and then concealed themselves until night-fall. From the position they had taken up they could see the glow of a fire in a 'cabin' in the glen, and as soon as dawn came they attacked it. Desmond was alone but for a single servant and, unable to defend himself properly because of his earlier injury, was wounded again by one of the Castlemaine soldiers.

Unaware who his attacker was, Desmond cried out, 'I am the Earl of Desmond! Save my life!', to which Owen is said to have replied: 'Thou has killed thyself long ago, and now thou shalt be prisoner to the Queen's Majesty and the Earl of Ormonde, Lord General of Munster'. As Desmond was unable to walk, Owen ordered his men to carry him but then, so he claimed later, fearing that the Earl might be rescued, he ordered one of his men to cut off his head. There is doubt as to the reasoning behind this since it would have suited the English administration to have Desmond returned alive to be tried for treason and duly executed. Instead they were handed his head, which was sent first to Ormond, who then duly sent it on to the Queen who had it put over the entrance to London Bridge, the usual place for displaying the heads of traitors.

Then in 1584 Sir Nicholas Malby died suddenly. Although he was capable of acting with great severity, by the time of his death he had achieved a certain amount of grudging respect in Connaught. Indeed the *Annals of the Four Masters* state: 'There came not to Eirinn in his own time, or often before, a better gentleman of the Foreigners than he', though they add that 'he placed all Connaught under bondage'. His death left a power vacuum for, as was the case following the recall of Sir

Henry Sidney, there was a prolonged period without a new appointment to the post of Lord Deputy. Finally, towards the end of 1584, the Queen and her advisers chose Sir John Perrot, who had considerable experience of the problems he was likely to face as he had earlier been President of Munster. Possibly the people of Connaught looked more favourably on Malby with hindsight than they had when he was alive because of Perrott's appointment as the new Governor of Connaught of Sir Richard Bingham, the man who would become notorious for his cruelty throughout the length and breadth of the country.

It was Perrott who, in September 1585, supervised the drawing up of the document, *The Composition of Connaught*, and, if further proof were needed that Richard-an Iarainn was still alive, it is that it is Perrott's name which heads the document which treats with him and which specifically sets out the terms of the MacWilliam succession. The reasons behind the drawing up of the document are complex, as is the nature of its content, so what follows is the basic information necessary to continue with the story.

There are two drafts of the document, one dated 4 September 1585 and the other 13 September, though both appear to be identical. The document opens: 'Indenture between the Rt. Hon Sir John Perrott (Knight), Lord Deputy, on behalf of the Queen and Sir Richard Bourke, otherwise called the McWilliam Eyghter, and many others including William Bourke of Ballencastel, otherwise called the Blind Abbot'. There follows a whole string of names including Molaghan O'Mayle of Belclare, otherwise called 'the O'Mayle, the chief of his clan, Teige Roe O'Mayl of Cahairenmart, Owen O'Mayle of the same . . .'

It sets out that the whole country and territory of Mayo is divided into nine principal baronies (and lists them) followed by pages and pages detailing the acreage and 'quarters' involved in order to calculate Crown rents. It continues: 'The said lords and chieftains, etc. acknowledging the manifold benefits and easements they find in possessing of their lands and goods, since the peaceable government of the said Lord Deputy, and the just dealings of Sir Richard Bingham (knight), do grant to the Queen's most excellent Majesty and her heirs, one yearly rent charge of ten shillings of good and lawful current money, going out for every quarter, which the whole amounteth yearlie to some £600 sterling and for any lack of money the thresurer (sic) or general receiver shall receive kyne [cattle] to the value of the said rent and do covenant to bear yearlie and forever, to all hostings, rood and journies within the said province of Connaught and Thomond, forty good and able horsemen and two hundred footmen well armed and furnished with arms, garras and victuals, and fifteen good able horsemen and fifty footmen to all general hostings proclaimed in this realm.

'The Lord Deputy and aforesaid lords, chieftains, etc. covenant, promise and agree that Sir Richard Bourke, otherwise called MacWilliam Eughter, in respect of the ancientie of his name and for better support and maintenance of the degree of knighthood whereunto it hath pleased the Queen to call him, shall have by letters patent [there follows a lengthy list of castles and lands] and that he and his heirs shall hold the same of the Queen by the twentieth part of a Knight's fee, as of her manor or howse of Strade in the said county, one faire chief horse, yearly to be presented in her Majesty's name to the Lord Deputy with these words engraven in gold: *"unde veni redeo"*.'

The most significant part of the document with regard to Richard-an-Iarainn comes at the end: 'Provided also, where there appeareth certain emulacion or envy betwixt the the above-named McWilliam Eyghter and his kins-

men, whereof there are some compettytours (sic) and that
by reason of their byrth be descended of MacWilliams of
greater fame and reputacion than the said Sir Richard
Bourke and think themselves more worthy of the English
succession now devised by this Composicion, and other
standings upon the expectancy of succeeding in his place,
wishes the continuance of that costomary name, that it
shall rest in the consideracion of the Lord Deputie for
the time being, how, and in what sort, the above-named
castles, manors, rents and signorys belonging to the name
of Macwilliam, shall be disposed or limited to the said
MacWilliam and his heirs said kynsmen. Dated this 13th
day of September Anno Domini 1585.'

Early in 1586 Richard-an-Iarainn did die, apparently
of natural causes, having enjoyed the chieftainship for
which his mother had been prepared to commit murder
on his behalf, for only a few brief years. The English
succession law applied and Tibbot jointly succeeded with
his two elder stepbrothers to his father's estate at
Burrishoole. Widowed a second time, Grace was under
no illusion as to what would happen next, and promptly
gathering together all her followers and taking with her
a thousand head of cattle and horses, she left at once for
Rockfleet, claiming, from then on, that it had become
hers by right.

While nothing can excuse the savagery with which the
English dealt with any hint of rebellion in Ireland, it
had its roots in what as happening on the mainland
where Elizabeth had come increasingly under threat.
Reading the reports in the State Papers of the late 1570s
and early to mid-1580s and the reports and letters passing between London and Dublin, one is struck by what
appears to be almost an obsession with regard to the part
played by the Scots in Ireland. They are mentioned
continually. Great concern is expressed at the numbers

of those settling permanently on the north-east coast and the very large numbers who are ferried over every year for the fighting season. Hundreds, indeed sometimes thousands, of Scots are reported as taking part in any uprising or battle of note, and one of the first things a conquered chieftain is ordered to do, as we have seen in the case of Richard-an-Iarainn and his rebellion, is to get rid of the Scots, preferably sending them back home to Scotland.

It was not simply because of their fighting prowess, for which the English had a healthy respect, it was also because of the long shadow cast by Mary Stewart, still held prisoner in England. Excommunicated and with the need for her assassination heartily endorsed by the Pope, Elizabeth was faced with an accelerating series of plots aimed at putting Mary on the English throne. Indeed there were two, the Somerville and Throgmorton, in 1582 alone. On each occasion when the plot was discovered, although pressed hard by her advisers to do so, Elizabeth had refused to act against her cousin, not least, she said, because she had no absolute proof that Mary had been party to what was going on. In actual fact it was more complicated than that. Elizabeth was only too well aware that while Mary lived, her own life would always be at risk, but by executing Mary she was not only shedding family blood but authorising the death of an anointed sovereign who had become Queen by Divine Right.

If what would finally force the Queen to act was cast-iron proof, then, in desperation, Walsingham determined to give it to her. While he and Elizabeth's other great adviser, William Cecil, Lord Burleigh, rarely saw eye to eye, they were unanimous where Mary was concerned: the only way to remove the threat to the throne she would always pose was to dispose of her once and for all.

So when intelligence reached Walsingham that yet

another plot was afoot, its ringleader a young and naive Catholic country landowner called Sir Anthony Babbington, he made his move, which was to infiltrate an *agent provocateur* into the circle of what it was clear were amateur plotters. The man he chose for the job was his very best intelligencer, Robert Poley, a master spy and a possible double agent, the doubt being that his part in subsequent events was so devious that a case could be made that he had been playing off both sides for his own ends.

Soon he was not only encouraging the conspirators but had made himself so necessary to Mary that she was trusting him with the plotters' correspondence. One man, Thomas Morgan, did warn the others that Poley, so anxious, so eager, might well be a plant but his advice was ignored. Soon all the correspondence to and from Mary was being intercepted, copied and, when in code, deciphered. Finally Walsingham decided he had enough evidence. The dénouement came when Poley invited all the conspirators to a supper party at his house and although, through sheer incompetence, they were not all picked up then, within days they were all in custody, Babbington believing in Poley until the very end. Under torture Ballard, one of the conspirators, betrayed the rest and the unfortunate men, after being found guilty of treason, were dragged on hurdles to Tyburn and hanged, drawn and quartered. In February of the following year Mary, Queen of Scots, went to the block at Fotheringay.

That at least was one threat the less but now, looming over everything, was the very real threat of a Spanish invasion. The Spaniards had already overrun the Low Countries. Would the invasion be mounted from Ireland? Of the two previous attempts, one might have been incompetent and the second derisory, but both had involved a landing first in Ireland. Now all the news from Europe and the intelligence of Walsingham's spies were pointing to King Philip of Spain mounting a major offensive, one which was neither incompetent nor derisory, but which would be backed up by an enormous armada and thousands of men.

For a brief while Connaught, like the rest of the country, remained quiet for various reasons. Firstly, Sir John Perrott, while agreeing to pursue the policy of the English government, preferred negotiation to confrontation whenever possible. Secondly, the long years of the Desmond rebellion had left all the participants exhausted. But Richard Bingham was soon to change all that. Bingham, born in Dorset, had been schooled for the military life from an early age and had perhaps fought against the Scots, and certainly against the Spanish in the Low Countries. He had also been part of the force that took part in the massacre at Smerwick, and shortly after his appointment, in spite of the relative peace, he had been involved in fights with marauding bands of Scots.

Seen from London, Bingham's appointment might well have seemed a sensible one, that of a tough, pragmatic soldier who would ensure all was kept under control, but in almost every other way he proved to be a disaster and has passed into Irish folklore as a cross between Genghis Khan and Bluebeard. As one commentator puts it, 'he was cruel, harsh and cunning, out to enrich himself at all costs and exterminate the natives . . .' This may be somewhat over the top, but he certainly has little to commend him. He figures so prominently in the events of the next few years that he comes across as a giant of a fellow, towering over his opponents, whereas in reality he was a small man, which, if other examples are anything to go on, might do something to explain his behaviour. From the start he had little sympathy with those he had been appointed to govern. 'The Irish', he said, 'were never tamed with words but with swords.'

There is no record of how Grace spent the time immediately after her return to Rockfleet though, once again, legends abound. A couple are of interest, not because they may or may not be true but because in view of what was to come they seem prophetic in that they show Grace in defeat. The first concerns the McEvilly brothers who had already fallen out with each other (one suspected the other of sleeping with his wife) as well as falling out with Grace who had turfed one of them out of his castle by, the storyteller says somewhat gnomically, 'a stratagem unworthy of a heroine'. She then demanded that the other, Hobburt, pay her a yearly tribute of a barrel of meal, a fat pig and an ox for every family on his estate.

She then sent her steward to Hobburt, at Luffertaun Castle, to collect her dues. But Hobburt considered himself too much of a 'gentleman' to pay tribute to a woman and said to the steward: 'I am here and she is below me and I will give her nothing'. The steward duly brought back the message and Grace immediately sent a party of men back to Luffertaun again, charged with collecting Hobburt's head and bringing it to her. They arrived at the castle to be told that Hobburt could not see them for he was at his prayers and could not be disturbed until he had finished them. Grace's men were determined not to be thwarted and attempted to go upstairs in spite of the efforts of his servants to prevent them, but one of them called out to Hobburt's three sons, who were out with the ploughmen in the fields to the east of the castle, and they came running to his aid. At this Grace's men ran away and Owen MacEgan, who was carrying the hatchet with which to cut off Hobburt's head, leapt over a river, leaving it behind as he jumped. Hobburt's three sons hotly pursued him. The youngest, having seized the hatchet and outrun his two brothers, caught up with Owen and struck off his head with the very weapon intended for his father. After this Grace left the MacEvillys severely alone.

In the second legend, Grace is said to have brought her men up to Burren in County Clare and laid siege to the castle of O'Loughlin Burren. A cannonball, aimed at her, tore up the ground under her feet and she was heard to say: 'May you be worse this day twelve month. It is well you have not knocked me down'. O'Loughlin's men then appeared on all sides to relieve the castle and took off their blankets. When Grace saw the rocky hills of Burren covered with men stripped to their white shirts, she retreated.

The reality was to be much worse, for Bingham's activities in Connaught would spark off a rebellion which would draw in two of her sons, leaving one dead and one a hostage, and herself facing execution. For Bingham, Grace had become a personal enemy.

10

Drawing in the Scots –
the Shadow of the Gallows

Bingham's activities were eventually to open up a gulf
between himself and Perrott which would never again
be bridged; in fact Perrott was collecting evidence of his
brutality which he intended handing to the English
government. However, as recorded in the *Annals of the
Four Masters*, 'the greater part of the people of Ireland
were, at this time, obedient to their Sovereign', and this
being the case, on 26 April the Irish Parliament was
reconvened, its House of Commons made up of three
elements: the old Anglo-Irish, the Gaelic Irish, and
English officialdom. The formal opening was a splendid
affair and it was said that all who attended were
impressed by the dignity of Sir John Perrott and the
splendour of his robes.

But unsurprisingly the peace was not to last, not even
in the Parliament. Perrott, while he might have achieved
some kind of respect and even popularity among some
of the Irish, not least the O'Neills, was loathed by his
own civil servants and heartily disliked by the Anglo-
English within the Pale who opposed all he did. They
particularly resented his attack on a new Act, Poyning's
Act, specifically designed to limit the authority of the
Lord Deputy, which Perrott promptly repealed. Racked
by acrimony, less than four weeks later the Parliament
was dissolved and never met again until after the Queen's
death in 1603.

While it might have seemed to Grace and Richard that

the *Composition of Connaught* had finally settled the matter of the MacWilliam succession which would then, under English law, pass to one of Richard's sons, it did no such thing and neither Tibbot, nor either of his elder brothers, succeeded to the chieftainship. There had, after all, been a clause in the document suggesting the possibility that a claim to it might in the future come from a contender who felt he had more right to it and that the matter would then have to be settled by the administration. Unfortunately, after Richard's death there were two immediate claimants, Richard Oliverus (as might have been expected), but also the elderly Edmund Burke of Castlebar, father-in-law to Grace's son, Owen. There was also growing disquiet over the number of chieftains who had still not signed up to the *Composition*, not least because they had no wish endorse the phrase 'the just dealings of Sir Richard Bingham', and mong them were Grace's two sons by Donal, Owen and Murrough O'Flaherty.

One of Bingham's tasks as governor was to ensure that all the conditions of the *Composition* were properly implemented. This was not considered to be a particularly onerous task as, on the whole and barring a few exceptions like the O'Flaherties, the document had been found largely acceptable and the new system of collecting rents considerably fairer than the old system of 'cess'. However, not all could have gone smoothly for we learn, quite casually, that Bingham held a 'session' (presumably a court) in Galway early in 1586 which resulted in the hanging of seventy people, including members of several leading families.

Then, in February, a major row broke out among the MacWilliams over the right to the succession, Edmund Bourke now formally claiming the title as his own. He refused to have the matter resolved by the administration and he, accompanied by a number of minor chiefs, set up base in Castle Hag on Lough Mask. There they were joined by Grace's son-in-law, 'the Devil's Hook', Richard Bourke and, shortly afterwards, by Grace herself. Determined to settle the revolt quickly, Bingham decided to launch his attack on the conspirators by boat. It was a mistake he almost didn't live to regret, for it resulted in his nearly drowning himself and most of his men. It took him some time to recover and while he was doing so and deciding what to do next, his quarries escaped, ferried over the water by Grace. He would never forgive her for making him look such a fool.

He then tried a different ploy, that of divide and rule. He offered safe conduct for any of those who wished to treat with him, and Richard Roe Bourke (who had not taken part in the actual rebellion), and the sons of Walter Fada Bourke, took him at his word, went to meet him and were promptly hanged, a ruse he would use again. After that it looked as if the revolt might now be over. It is impossible to firm up the dates but either immediately before the revolt, or during the early stages of it, Bingham took Tibbot hostage, sending him off to his brother George, who was Sheriff of Sligo, for safekeeping. George actually treated him well, and while he was in captivity Tibbot learned both to read and write in English, skills he would later put to good use.

Even more confusing, it was also about this time that Tibbot got married although there is no recorded date and it is likely that the marriage took place immediately after his imprisonment. His bride was Maeve O'Connor Sligo, 'Maeve of the yellow-gold hair', and since we have been told of his golden curls and blue eyes, they must have made a handsome couple. It was considered an excellent match, for the O'Connors had once been kings of Connaught and High Kings of Ireland. While records suggest that in reality Tibbot was a well-educated and civilised, if tough, young man, folklore is less kind.

A note in *A Choreographical Description of West Connaught*
states that Maeve 'had but little comfort with Tibbot, as
he was proud, rude, tyrannical and barbarous. Many
anecdotes are still remembered of him which show he
was a very rude warrior and in every way particularly
worthy of his mother, Grainne'. This is followed by a
number of repetitive instances in which he is alleged to
have treated his wife badly. There is, however, no proof
of this.

As all was quiet, in an effort to prevent further rebellion and bloodshed Perrott decided it was time and more
to make peace with the Macdonalds, particularly Sorley
Boy Macdonald, who was now an old man. In June 1586,
on Perrott's invitation, he came to Dublin to be greeted
by the sight of the head of his son, Alastair, killed in a
skirmish with the English, spiked above the Castle gate.
He stood and looked at it, then told Perrott proudly that
he 'had other sons'. However, he made his submission, in
front of a portrait of the Queen, admitted his past deeds
and declared himself to be from now on her faithful
subject. He was given lands by Letters Patent, as were
members of his family, for which he had to promise that
neither he nor his heirs would ever retain 'more than
thirty Scots' in their households.

In July trouble again broke out among the various
MacWilliam septs which, coupled with hatred for
Bingham, resulted in what was to become known as the
second Bourke rebellion. This time the Bourkes were
joined by the O'Malleys, the Gibbons, the Joyces and,
'secretly' it is said (though on what grounds is not made
clear), by Richard 'the Devil's Hook' and this time also
by Grace and the recently released Tibbot. Soon news
reached Bingham that the Bourkes were awaiting the
arrival of a formidable force of Redshanks to help them
launch an attack, so on 12 July he marched against the
Bourkes and their allies determined to put an end to the

revolt before their arrival. A parley was suggested but this failed because, according to Bingham, the chieftains flatly refused to accept the Queen's rule. He immediately proclaimed all the rebels traitors and executed the hostages he was holding. Learning that the Redshanks were likely to arrive any time and realising he had not a sufficient force to take them on, he rounded up as many of the rebels' cattle as he could, slaughtering those he did not take away with the intention of ensuring that the Bourkes would be left without any means of paying for, and thus employing, the Scots.

But Bingham's efforts did not stop there. Grace's son Owen was, as noted earlier, married to Edmund Bourke's daughter but there is no proof that he himself had taken any part in the rebellion. But whether he had or not, Bingham had him as a marked man and Owen's subsequent actions would lead to his death. It is hardly surprising, however, that the accounts of the two people most closely involved, Grace and Bingham, are completely at odds as to how and why it happened.

According to Grace, as quoted in Privy Council State Papers seven years later, Owen, learning that a substantial force under the captaincy of Richard Bingham's brother, John, were on their way to the barony of Ballinahinch in search of victualling for the men, ferried his cattle and horses over to an island north of Bunowen and hid them 'for their better assurance'. John Bingham duly arrived, accompanied by five hundred men, and camped out on the mainland opposite the island, demanding that Owen should give up some of his cattle to feed them. Faced by such a force, Owen agreed to do a deal over the cattle, after which he naively ferried John Bingham and his men over to the island in his own boats to discuss the matter in more detail, entertaining them as best he could.

But in the middle of the night John Bingham ordered

his troops to seize Owen and eighteen of his most trusted men and bind them securely. As soon as dawn broke, Bingham's men ferried ashore some 4000 cows, 500 horses and a thousand sheep, leaving the inhabitants of the island stripped and helpless. John Bingham then sent for Owen and his followers and 'that evening he caused the said eighteen persons, without trial or good cause, to be hanged among whom was hanged a gentleman of land and living called Thebault O' Twohill being of the age of four score and ten years. The next night following, a false alarm was raised in the camp and in the dead of night, the said Owen being fast bound . . . at that instant the said Owen was cruelly murdered, having twelve deadly wounds, and in that miserable sort he ended his years and unfortunate days'.

Sir Richard Bingham's version, also recorded in the relevant State Papers when he was later charged (among other serious matters) with having been complicit in the murder, is that Owen was no more nor less than an 'open rebel' and therefore could be treated as such. As to his death, Bingham then fell back on the excuse used by such people throughout recorded history right up to the present day: that Owen, having been taken prisoner by his brother, had somehow managed to escape and 'in pursuit was slain because he would not stand or yield himself'.

For most of that summer Bingham had been tied up fighting Scots. The Redshanks invited by the Bourkes had not been deterred from coming either by the harsh treatment meted out by Bingham or the lack of money caused by his having stolen or killed so many of the cattle which represented the clan's wealth, and a force of between 1400 and 1500 of them had landed at Lough Foyle looking for trouble. News soon reached Bingham and on 28 August he set off to intercept them before they could do any harm, having with him '400 foot, of whom 300 were Irish but lately enrolled, sixty horse and 200 kerne', to discover that the Redshanks had now been joined by a considerable number of Irish reinforcements. Realising that he was unlikely to win any immediate confrontation, he decided on a cat-and-mouse game. The position in which the Scots were encamped was such that they would eventually be forced to leave it or starve, by which time (given some reinforcements) Bingham could take them on in the open country, which would be to his advantage.

For two weeks he sat it out until, on a night of strong wind and heavy rain, the Scots outwitted him, rushing the bridge over the Owenmore River, Bingham's Irish troops having fled at the sight of them. Four hundred got across the bridge before Bingham had properly realised what was happening, while the rest crossed the river at a ford unknown to him. As the State Papers put it: 'They [the Scots] were loose in Connaught and he did not know which way they were going'.

Baulked of his prey and with no end in sight to the Bourke revolt, Bingham made his next move. Grace was in Burrishoole preparing to sail to Ulster to bring in further reinforcements of Scots and to that end was in the middle of negotiations with the O'Donnell chief in Donegal. The O'Donnell was suspected of mischief even by Sir John Perrott who reported to the Queen that he (O'Donnell) was always 'ready to send aid to any that were evil disposed in your kingdom, as of late he did to Grany ne Male to see if they would make any stir in Connaught'.

Bingham decided the time had come to get his own back on the woman who had organised the escape from Lough Mask, that nurse of all rebellions and drawer-in of the Scots, and sent her word that for her own safety she should leave Burrishoole at once and to that end promised her safe conduct. It seems almost unbelievable that she actually believed him, but for whatever reason she did and set off, presumably for Rockfleet, with a small party of men and some cattle. As soon as she reached open country she was met by 'five bands of men under the leading of Captain John Bingham'. They took the cattle, then, after she had been securely bound hand and foot, John Bingham delivered his prisoner to his brother. The reason Bingham gave for acting when he did was that Grace had once again raided the Arran Islands.

She could have been under no illusions this time as to what was in store. To ram the message home that he brooked no opposition, Bingham promptly executed all the hostages he had in his charge, among them Moyler and Tibbot Reagh Bourke, first cousins to Tibbot. Also hanged were those in the charge of the sheriff, among them Ullick, the son of the William Bourke known, as in the *Composition of Connaught*, as 'the Blind Abbot'. All had been accused, as noted in State Papers, of 'drawing in the Scots', whether it was true or not. But for whatever reason Bingham did not execute Grace straight away, keeping her in prison for several weeks until he finally decided to make an example of her.

Amid much publicity, a special gallows was built for the event. As she was to say herself later, she felt all hope was at an end and that she was preparing 'for her last funeral'. We then learn that against all the odds and Bingham's previous record, she was reprieved on the very day execution was to take place, on the pledge of her son-in-law, Richard Bourke, even though 'the Devil's Hook' was supposedly known to be secretly supporting the rebellion. This stretches belief to breaking point. It seems incredible that Bourke, a man heavily involved in the previous revolt, was somehow able to convince Bingham that he should cancel the execution of his mother-in-law merely by pledging his word for her good behaviour, after which Bingham simply handed her over: a woman who Bingham truly, if wrongly, believed had been behind every revolt in Connaught for the last forty years. Not only that, but Bourke's current activities could hardly have been a secret, for immediately on Grace's release he openly joined the rebels again.

Information from Trinity College suggests a different, though equally puzzling, sequence of events: that at the last moment, when Grace was either about to climb up on to the gallows or was actually standing on them, a messenger arrived in the nick of time bearing a Royal Warrant for her release and that Bingham therefore had no alternative but to set her free. If this is the case, then once again we are left wondering, as with her previous release from imprisonment, why it happened. On that first occasion there had also been some kind of unspecified intervention. Was it possible that while she was more than prepared (particularly following Owen's murder) to fight the English in general and Bingham in particular on land, she was still prepared to pass on information on shipping movements to a far higher authority than the Lord Deputy? Was the pledge of the Devil's Hook used as a cover? The minds and methods of those engaged in intelligence-gathering, espionage, and counter-espionage have changed little during succeeding centuries and Walsingham was a past master in such black arts. Given the now overt threat from Spain, if Grace was considered to be more useful alive than dead, then Bingham's desire for vengeance would count for very little. It is unlikely we will ever know the truth, but either way Grace was released – and promptly set about drawing in more Scots, setting off with her galleys to Ulster to bring in further reinforcements.

Bingham was now determined to end the Bourke rebellion. He learned that the hundreds of Redshanks who had escaped into Connaught had now regrouped and had set up camp at Ardnaree, opposite Ballina on the River Moy. If the revolt was to be put down, then they must be destroyed. Bingham therefore raised the largest force he could and crossed the Slieve Gamph mountains in search of them. On 22 September, while they were sleeping, he mounted a surprise attack with every man and weapon at his disposal. The Scots, roused from sleep and quite unprepared, fought bravely but Bingham outflanked them, sending his horsemen into them. For the Scots, with their backs to the river, it ended in disaster. Both the sons of James Macdonald of the Isles, Donald Gorme and Alexander Carragh Macdonald, were killed.

'I was never,' wrote Captain Thomas Woodhouse, one of those taking part, 'so weary of killing men; for I protest to God, for as fast I could I did but hough them and paunch them, sometimes on horseback, because they did run as we did brake them and sometimes on foot.' There must have been country people living nearby and possibly also camp followers, even children present, for apart from about eighty men, women and children who managed to escape by swimming across the Moy River, all the rest were put to the sword. As Cyril Falls comments in *Elizabeth's Irish Wars*, 'Whatever may be thought of his conduct from the moral point of view, he [Bingham] had here read a lesson which was as effective as it was terrible and which was to be long remembered'. To mark the end of the Bourke rebellion Bingham hanged the elderly Edmund Bourke, Owen O'Flaherty's father-in-law, whose claim to become the MacWilliam had been a root cause of it.

Although it was now supposedly over, Grace was taking no chances and spent the winter and spring of 1587 in Ulster. She had set off north with a number of galleys, possibly to ferry Scots either to or from the mainland, when she ran into exceptionally bad weather. Her ostensible reason for remaining so long in Ulster was the extent of the repairs needed to her fleet following the storm. But it is likely there was more to it than that, not least self-preservation. In view of what had happened in Connaught, the greater distance between herself and Bingham, the better.

The prolonged visit would also enable her to talk at length with the O'Neill, Turlough Luineach, his ambitious and clever tanist, Hugh, and with the chief of the O'Donnells. One subject must have been that of the coming Spanish invasion, what their position would be if it succeeded, whether it would be better or worse than being ruled by the English, how they should react, who would sit on the English throne now the obvious contender was dead. Grace must also have been impressed at how Ulster had been far more successful in keeping English forces and English laws at bay compared with elsewhere, and how they had escaped the fate of Munster after the Desmond rebellion: the destroyed towns and villages, the burning of crops and killing of cattle, the slow starvation of those who were not put to the sword or hanged; and more recently in Connaught, Bingham's putting down of the Bourke revolt, his deviousness and cruelty, his massacre not only of the Scots, but of women and children as well, a man whose savagery knew no bounds, who had murdered her son and been prepared to hang her.

By now relations between Sir John Perrott and Bingham had reached breaking point. A steady stream of complaints against Bingham had been flowing to London, apart from the dossier compiled by Perrott. Unfortunately the Privy Council, aware of the now open enmity between the two men and unwilling to take action at such a time against so skilled a military man, acquitted Bingham of the various charges made against him, but at least for the time being he was recalled, before being sent off to fight in the Low Countries. Perrott believed he had seen the last of Bingham but when he was later told that in the course of time Bingham would be sent back to Ireland, he immediately asked to be relieved of his post, and in 1588 his place was taken by Sir William Fitzwilliam. The Bourke rebellion had been the last flare-up of revolt during his time as Lord Deputy and at the time he left Ireland, all was quiet. He had made some powerful friends and it is said that as his ship sailed away for England the old Tirlagh O'Neill watched it go with tears in his eyes.

There is a sad footnote to Perrott's personal history. He had always been considered a loyal and faithful servant of the Queen but was known for speaking his mind, especially when annoyed, and was quite prepared to criticise those above him, even the Queen. After the defeat of the Armada, he was wrongly accused of treason on the strength of a forged letter bearing his forged signature, in which he was supposed to have pledged his loyalty to King Philip of Spain, offering to assist him in his takeover of England and Ireland. This led to the further accusation that he had shown sympathy and favour to Papist traitors during his time as Lord Deputy in Ireland. He was put in the Tower and in 1592 stood trial for treason and was found guilty. But the Queen, shocked that matters had got that far and clearly not believing the verdict, refused to sign his death warrant and was proposing to pardon him when he died of natural causes. The forged letter is thought to have been the work of a Charles Trevor, who then fled to Scotland. One wonders if his arch-enemy Bingham had a hand in it.

But immediately before Perrott left and while he was still Lord Deputy, Grace, learning that Bingham had been recalled to England, left Ulster for Dublin to beg Sir John to grant her an Official Pardon. She must have been convincing for it is recorded in State Papers that she did indeed receive it at his hands. The Pardon was granted for all past offences against the Crown, and also included in it were her sons Murrough O'Flaherty and Tibbot and her daughter, Margaret. Once again she was off the hook.

11

The Spanish Armada

Rejoice unto the Lord with mirth,
Which us, from foreign fears
Preserved hath in quiet state
These eight and twenty years.

These words, set to music by William Byrd, were sung
heartily during celebrations for the Queen's reign in 1586
in gratitude that the Lord had brought the nation peace
'through his handmaid Elizabeth'; it is highly unlikely
they would have been echoed in Ireland. But by 1587 few
people were under any illusion as to what was to come.
However, Elizabeth and her advisers had every reason to
believe that even – or when – an invasion did take place,
the Catholics were unlikely to give it the support they
might have done had Mary Stewart still been alive. From
the purely pragmatic point of view Walsingham had
been right to force the issue.

Nor was there likely to be much enthusiasm at the
prospect of the King of Spain grabbing hold of the crown
for himself as was his stated aim. Indeed he had employed
a team of genealogists to prove that he had a hereditary
right to the English throne and they claimed to have
proved it through the family of John of Gaunt. To be
quite certain, he announced that Mary Stewart, facing
death, had bequeathed it to him. Even in the unlikely
event that he had been able to substantiate his claim it
is still almost beyond belief that he would have been

welcomed except by a handful of fanatics. While more than a generation had passed since his disastrous marriage to Mary Tudor, the memory of the fires of Smithfield still burned deep in the consciousness of the people.

The appointment of Sir William Fitzwilliam as the new Lord Deputy for Ireland was announced in February 1588. He was sixty-two years old and had been Governor of Fotheringay at the time of Mary Queen of Scots' execution and was known to have treated her throughout her imprisonment with respect. He has been described as a pessimist, always looking on the dark side, but he was also considered a man of sound judgement and common sense. He was to need both for during the spring of 1588 Sir Richard Bingham was again appointed Governor of Connaught.

History now shows that Spain had been planning to mount an invasion of England in 1587. A report in the *State Papers of Ireland* notes that an Irish sailor called Miles Brewitt, who had landed in Lisbon, was taken before the Spanish Admiral, the Marques de Santa Cruz, and questioned closely about the activities and whereabouts of Sir John Perrott, the Marques claiming him as an old acquaintance even though he was 'a great Lutheran'. Apparently he had hoped to acquire one of the horses and one of the hawks for which Perrott was famous.

The Admiral treated Brewitt affably and asked after the state of Ireland, to which the sailor had replied that it had never been quieter, adding – or so he alleged when questioned later – that he had also told the Admiral that it was strongly fortified. While in Lisbon he also met up with the son of James Fitzmaurice who told him that King Philip had promised him 5,000 troops to mount an invasion from Ireland and that he had it on good authority that, except for those living in the Pale, Waterford and Cork, the rest of the population would welcome and recognise Philip II as their King. Cyril Falls, in *Elizabeth's Irish Wars*, points out that this might well have been the ideal time to do it as there were only 1,761 English troops in the Irish list and the armaments were in a parlous state, the guns rusty, their carriages rotting for lack of maintenance, and supplies of powder and small arms deficient. But using Ireland as a launching pad would have been both hazardous and unnecessary.

King Philip had indeed seen the spring or summer of 1587 as his best window of opportunity and he had been assured of success. He was much influenced by an English priest, William Allen (later made a Cardinal), who had established a college first at Douai, then at Rheims, for the training of student missionary priests to be sent to England. (In passing, it is very likely that it was the role of just such a missionary priest that was assumed by the poet and dramatist Christopher Marlowe when spying for Walsingham in the early 1590s.) In any event it is obvious that either King Philip's intelligencers were nothing like as talented as those of Walsingham or, as with many other powerful people before and since, he was told only what he wanted to hear. According to Allen, every honest Englishman wanted nothing better than to see the flag of Spain flying over the Tower and English Catholics could not wait to welcome him.

There was no question at this time of mounting anything like the Armada that was launched a year later. The large vessels of the Spanish fleet were to be used to convey the Duke of Parma and the high command, carry the heavy armaments and convey across the Channel some 17,000 Spanish troops from the Low Countries. The planned landing was to be close to the Thames estuary. In fact what was proposed was a land, not a sea, war. The delay in putting the plan into action, however, is largely down to Sir Francis Drake and his raids on Cadiz and Corunna when he set fire to a large number of Spanish ships being prepared for the event. He also brought home as a prize the *San Philip*, one of the richest prizes ever to fall into English hands.

With fear of invasion so much in the air, when Fitzwilliam took up the post of Lord Deputy he was promised that, should the need arise, 10,000 men could quickly be landed in Ireland by the English fleet. He issued a statement to that effect from Dublin but at the same time made it known that he would rather have had 3-4,000 men on the spot there and then, as this might well put the Spaniards off the idea altogether. If any attempt was made to land, however, English policy was simple. Every effort must be made to hunt down and kill any Spaniard who came ashore, and there would be no taking of prisoners. As this was widely known in Spain, history shows, as Falls points out, that if Ireland was the last place where the English wanted to see Spaniards, it was also the last place to which Spaniards wanted to go. 'The Captain General, when he set his course for the north, had no thought of the possible advantages of landing several thousand troops in Ireland; he simply wanted to get back to Spain, dreading the dangerous Irish west coast.'

There are no mentions of Grace in any of the accounts of the time or what she was doing during the weeks immediately after the defeat of the Armada, though there are references to the activities of the O'Malleys in general. But the effect of the disaster on Connaught and Bingham's Draconian reaction to it were to have such major repercussions on her and her family that if her history is to be followed further, it is necessary to know something of what happened in the aftermath of 1588.

So to the Armada. Immediately before its despatch to England, William, now Cardinal, Allen addressed an *Admonition to the Nobility and People of England*. The coming invasion, he informed them, which must have their support, was a Crusade to restore the Catholic religion and to rid them of their Queen, 'that monster of impiety and unchastity . . . [who] cannot be tolerated without the eternal infamy of our whole country, the whole world deriding our effeminate dastardy (sic), that have suffered such a creature for almost thirty years to reign over our bodies and souls'.

The summer of 1588 was a stormy one and July was no exception, but by the middle of the month it was full moon and visibility was good. Warned that an invasion attempt could be expected at any time, watchers had been posted on vantage points all around the coast and a series of beacons prepared to warn of the Armada's imminent approach. At three o'clock on the afternoon of 19 July watchers on the Lizard saw a terrifying sight, the might of Spain rising up before them over the horizon. Spanish ships had extraordinarily high superstructures: 'built high like towers and castles, [they] rallied into the form of a crescent whose horns were at least seven miles distant, coming slowly on . . .', according to William Camden.

The beacons were lit, the warning given. That Drake really did announce that he was going to finish his game of bowls before setting off to fight the Spaniards might well be just a myth (though try telling that to the people of Plymouth), but he was right in believing that on this occasion the English navy was fully prepared. At first Drake and Lord Howard, who was Admiral of the Fleet, deliberately held back from any kind of immediate engagement, allowing the Spaniards to sail on unchallenged. Shortly before nightfall the massive fleet anchored off Plymouth only to discover, when the moon rose at 2 a.m., that the English fleet had come up behind them. Most of what followed is well known, including the fact that the lean, low-built English ships had both speed and an ability to go about far faster than the lumbering Spanish galleons which found themselves at their mercy. There were three separate engagements on 23, 24 and 27 July, all of which inflicted heavy damage on the Spaniards who were pushed into the Calais Roads only to be set on there by Drake's fire ships. The worst battle was fought off Gravelines. A description of the close-packed Spanish galleons, top heavy and unable to escape the gunfire of the English fleet, tells of blood pouring from the ships' scuppers.

The crippled fleet was then driven towards the north of Scotland and on around the west coast of Ireland where the weather did the rest. The might of Spain was wrecked from end to end of the west coast of Ireland. Most of the vessels which did escape were under the command of the Duke of Medina Sidonia who had the common sense to ride out the storms at sea, well out to the west of Ireland. Gradually word filtered through, first to Dublin then to London, that hundreds, possibly thousands, of Spanish survivors were being washed up along the Irish coast. To the English this opened up the frightening possibility of countless Spaniards dispersing throughout Ireland to join with the Irish in any subsequent revolts. An immediate proclamation was issued to the effect that it was a crime punishable by death to hide or aid the enemy in any way. No exceptions would be made.

Soon wrecks were reported from Mayo and Donegal, the Dingle peninsula, the Aran Islands, the Shannon and Limerick estuaries and further north in Ulster. It is likely that there were five wrecks along the Mayo coast and there are a number of stories to the effect that the O'Malleys stripped both wreck and its survivors of everything of value, then despatched the latter. One such story concerns the galleon *El Gran Grin*, carrying 329 men, which became embayed in Clew Bay with the result that she was being blown helplessly on to a lee shore. Before she reached it, however, she was wrecked on Clare Island where it is said her captain, Don Pedro de Mendoza, and a hundred of his crew who had survived, managed to scramble to safety, only to be killed by the O'Malleys. A more upbeat Irish version is that the survivors were smuggled out of the country and taken to Scotland. Anne Chambers suggest that the *El Gran Grin* might have been the galleon that was wrecked close to Rockfleet and that the Clare island wreck was the *San Nicholas Prodaneli*. Whichever it was, the result was the same.

Three large ships entered Killybegs, only one of which, the *Girona*, was repairable. Here the survivors were treated well and the McSweeneys, the local galloglas, set about repairing the ship to enable them to escape. A little later they were joined by Medina Sidona's deputy Don Alonzo de Leyva and his men whose ship, *La Santa Maria Encoronada*, had been driven into Blacksod Bay on the Mayo coast and become a total wreck. Both he and his men survived this disaster as they had the good fortune to be taken off the shore by a transport vessel that had survived the storm. But this was, in turn, driven on to the rocks off Loughros Bay in Donegal, yet once again all were saved. The survivors then made their way over the mountains to Killybegs, carrying de Leyva who had been badly injured, where they discovered their compatriots awaiting completion of the repairs to the *Girona*. The McSweeneys did their best to make the ship seaworthy but it was soon apparent that the *Girona*, roughly repaired and overloaded, was unlikely to reach Spain and that the best bet was to make for the west coast of Scotland. But third time was not lucky for de Leyva and his crew. The patched-up ship hit more bad weather and was wrecked on rocks near Dunluce Castle with the loss of almost all those aboard.

The government's edict, proclaimed from Dublin by Fitzwilliam, meant exactly what it said and he led a mopping-up expedition to rid the country of every survivor. Indeed he even complained at one time that Bingham was not being tough enough in seeking them out and putting them to death. Bingham responded by informing him that his own brother had killed 700 Spaniards in Ulster alone and that he had hunted down and killed many more. Bingham told the Queen that he and his men had personally put to the sword some 1,100 in Connaught. On one occasion he agreed that he had spared some fifty officers with a view to ransoming them but that the Lord Deputy had ordered that these also be killed, including a number of unfortunate Dutchmen, impressed men, who had been forced to sail with the Spaniards, and that he had immediately carried out Sir William Fitzwilliam's order. Irish and English blame each other for the scale of the slaughter but there is no doubt that Bingham played a major role in it.

It was not only the military who took part in the killing. A small vessel was washed up in Tralee Bay with 24 survivors who were promptly captured by Lady Denny who lived nearby and were hanged, either by her or her husband.

In spite of the threat of the death penalty, there are a number of instances of the Irish assisting Spaniards to escape to Scotland. One such followed the wreck of the galleon *La Trinidad Valencera*, off Inishowen Island. There were 460 survivors who surrendered on the word of an officer called John Kelly. The officers were separated from the men and then either put to the sword or shot, but about 150 men escaped and were kindly treated by the O'Cahans and their chief, a vassal of the O'Neill, who passed them on to the Macdonalds in Antrim who ferried them to Scotland. They eventually ended up in Edinburgh where they were well treated and repatriated.

But the most remarkable story is that of Captain Don Francisco de Cuellar. He was the captain of a 24-gun galleon, the *San Pedro*, and was in the thick of the fighting throughout all three sea battles. On 10 August, having been without rest for ten days, he turned in while the pilot took the ship out of the line to effect running repairs, where he was joined by another vessel. Then either Medina Sidonia himself or, as some reports say, a senior captain called Don Francisco de Boradilla sent for de Cuellar and the captain of the other ship which had dropped out for repairs and sentenced them to death for deserting their posts, a charge which de Cuellar hotly denied, claiming that they had been made scapegoats. He had a lucky escape since his fellow-captain was indeed hanged.

Presumably de Cuellar was allowed back to his ship, for during the storm he was blown, with two other vessels, towards the Sligo coast. He tried to shelter near Rosses Point but all three were subsequently wrecked on Streadagh Strand. After being washed up on the beach, the survivors were 'fallen on by some 200 savages' who stripped them of everything, but de Cuellar managed to hide. When all was quiet, he returned to the beach to give his commander a decent burial but was himself set upon and robbed, one of his attackers being 'a savage damsel who hung [his valuables] around her neck, making me a sign she wished to keep them, saying she was a Christian; which was in like manner as was Mahommet!'

When dawn came, he set off in search of 'a monastery' but discovered that the nearest had been razed and burned, its images defaced. He had to hide from parties of Bingham's soldiers looking for survivors and once, finding a church which offered concealment, found twelve Spaniards hanging inside it. He claims that on one beach alone he found 400 bodies. He must have succeeded in keeping hold of some of his worldly goods, for he arrived at a village where he was set on by an old man, two youths and a girl 'most beautiful in the extreme', who robbed him of a gold chain. But another girl gave him butter, milk and oat bread and directed him 'over some mountains to the O'Rourkes', where he was met by a boy 'who knew some Latin', who gave him shelter and a horse. The O'Rourkes, when he reached them, were sympathetic, and gave him rest and dressed his wounds before passing him on to the McClancys, a vassal clan of the O'Rourkes.

The chief of the McClancys, who lived in Rossclogher Castle on an island in Lough Melvin on the Ulster border, was already sheltering eight other survivors. 'McClancy's wife and her ladies,' writes de Cuellar, 'conversed with me in Latin asking about Spain . . . they were beautiful, but badly dressed . . .' There is another story recorded in which a similar conversation takes place where the ladies are not dressed at all. A traveller, given hospitality by a chieftain, was offered the use of his 'sweat house', a kind of sauna. On taking up the offer, he found himself sitting inside it with four naked ladies who happily chatted to him, also in Latin.

But soon Bingham and Fitzwilliam were scouring the area for Spanish survivors and McClancy decided the most sensible course of action was to seek refuge in the mountains, taking his people, his cattle, and the Spaniards, with him. De Cuellar and the Spaniards decided to remain, de Cuellar offering to defend the castle which he thought would be difficult to take, surrounded as it was by deep water. There was also a plentiful supply of muskets and powder. The English force besieged the castle for seventeen days but finally gave up, gong off in search of easier quarry. When McClancy returned, he was so grateful that he offered de Cuellar his sister in marriage, an offer which de Cuellar respectfully declined. He and his compatriots then made their way across to Derry where 'Sorley Boy' Macdonald arranged for them to escape to Scotland. From

Scotland they were taken in a Dutch ship to Holland, and from there made their way home to Spain.

De Cuellar has left behind a highly entertaining account of his adventures in Ireland, and the way of life of the people he met. McClancy, on the other hand, was not so fortunate. Having finished his business elsewhere, and fully aware of what had happened at Lough Melvin, Bingham returned, hanged McClancy and sent his head to Dublin to be put on a spike over the Castle gate.

Even today no one knows exactly how many ships were wrecked off the Irish coast or, in many cases, where. In letters to Walsingham Bingham recorded what he himself knew of the Spanish losses in Connaught. Having described how the ships were driven ashore by the weather, he continues: 'there were by even portions, three ships in every of the four several counties bordering upon the sea coast, viz Sligo, Mayo, Galway and Thomond. So that 12 ships perished that we know of on the rocks and sands by the shore side, and also some three or four besides on the seaboards of the outer isles . . .'

Altogether 63 ships out of an Armada of 130 were lost, the fate of 35 being unknown. Only two were sunk during the running battles. A number were wrecked off the coasts of Holland, France, England and Scotland but the majority off Ireland. A likely figure is that 19 met their ends off the coasts of Donegal, Sligo, Galway, Mayo and Kerry. The estimate of the human loss is that some 5,394 men were drowned, killed or captured. It is possible that some survivors, successfully hidden from Fitzwilliam's troops, settled in Ireland and never went home. Both in Ireland and Cornwall there are those still said to be descendants of 'Armada' families, that is of children born of the union of a Spanish survivor and a local girl.

The major revolt that was to take place in Connaught in the aftermath of the Armada was almost entirely the result of the hunt-to-kill policy carried out by Fitzwilliam and Bingham in the months immediately after the catastrophe. Instead of allowing everything to settle down again, Bingham immediately turned his attention closer to home, accusing a number of Connaught chieftains, although he had no proof, of having harboured and succoured Armada survivors. Among those he accused were Richard Bourke, 'the Devil's Hook' and his son (Grace's grandson), an entire minor clan of Bourkes, those of Erris, and the old rebel, Sir Murrough-ne-Doe O'Flaherty, who very likely had and almost admitted as much.

The law stated that any clan chief later found to have done so would be considered a rebel and his lands forfeited to the Crown, and Bingham set out to implement it. Without Fitzwilliam's permission, he issued a Commission to John Browne, the sheriff of Mayo, giving him the power to enter the lands of the Burrishoole and Erris Bourkes and 'to prosecute and follow all and every one of the said traitors'. It would be quite lawful for him and his men to prey upon, burn and spoil all in their way, having warned them beforehand. Legally it was necessary for such a major commissioning document to be signed by two commissioners, a condition which Bingham ignored, his being the only signature on it.

An account in State Papers, dated 10 September 1589, describes the spark that lit the tinder in February, 'over Lent', that year. John Browne marched on Rockfleet with an army of between two and three hundred men. Since it was known to be Grace's stronghold, it is hardly likely to be a coincidence that it was Browne's first choice. Here he was met by Richard, 'the Devil's Hook's son'. Young Richard 'thought the coming into the country of such a number did not tend to any good end', not least because he had already heard rumours that Browne was gathering soldiers 'to go that way'. He therefore told Browne not to enter clan lands, telling him that 'all things that were due to her Majesty should not only be paid according to the Composition, but also all things else they ought to yield or pay'. In addition, 'for so doing he would give Browne himself 60 marks and a gold chain, which things the said Browne denied, saying he would go through their country and if they did think evil of that, he would drive them into the sea.

'Whereupon he [Browne] drew himself that night to Carrickhowlie and the next morning sent John Gilson, William Browne and Christopher Garvey, with a company to Irris [Erris] to gather the prey of the country, where they killed men, women and children, and himself the said Browne and Derbie Daly, with their companies followed, and took such preys as they found on the way. And the said Richard Bourke and his company, hearing of the killing aforesaid and the taking of their goods, met the said Browne and Daley with their company, assaulted them and killed them, as is heard and known . . .'

The report was from a Sir Arthur Clayton who had been invited to accompany the party but asked to see the necessary Commission 'to warrant our doings'. Unsurprisingly, in view of its dodgy legality, it wasn't shown to him. Indeed they told him if he was not prepared to trust them, 'I would see no Commission'. He therefore refused to go. He further declared that those murdered had been 'loyal tenants' and 'would have given them what was desired of them and trusted them as their own brothers and sisters'. Bingham's action in sending Browne into Mayo was indeed the match that set all Connaught aflame, the result being that the Lord Deputy was faced with a third, and by far the most serious, Bourke rebellion.

12

Rebellion

The ensuing revolt was to change Mayo forever yet, remarkably, it hardly merits more than a paragraph or two in most books on Irish history of the period, being treated as an unpleasant interlude between the destruction of the Armada and the rise of the O'Neills which was to end eventually in what became known as the Nine Years War.

Throughout Ireland, even today, Bingham is regarded as a sanguinary monster, and his massacre of women and children aroused the full wrath of the Bourkes. Five septs of the clan, together with O'Malleys, Clangibbons, plus the Clandonnell galloglas and, this time, Grace, Tibbot and his stepbrother, Edmund, were joined by Sir Murrough-ne-Doe O'Flaherty who crossed Lough Corrib to join them at the head of five hundred men. On hearing this, Bingham promptly hanged his son whom he had been holding hostage against his father's good behaviour.

As a result the rebels went south, burning and looting as they went. A frantic letter from the Mayor of Galway to the Lord Deputy (the original of which is in the British Library) tells how they 'had come and wasted, burned and destroyed all last week . . . Athenry castle has been put to ashes', along with the rest of the town including the abbey and church. They stopped at the walls of Galway and demanded that the city 'provide wine and other necessaries'. Fearful of what would happen if they didn't, the people of Galway had given them the supplies for which they asked 'apart from powder and shot'. Otherwise 'they would have come among us'. As it was, the rebels burned houses on the outskirts of Galway, which frightened the Mayor since the wind was blowing against the town, and loosed shot into it before riding off and 'burning every village down to the coast of Mayo'.

Grace's elder stepson, Walter, went into Costello and carried off, we are told, 'Theobald Dillon's goods and a gentleman who was in charge of them', and Grace, yet again, raided the Arran islanders; goodness knows what they had done to deserve her constant attention over the years. Though there is no doubt that by this time her control over the shipping lanes of the west coast was ebbing away, she had not given up piracy. As Knox writes in *The Early History of County Mayo*, 'she did not altogether give up her old trade of "maintenance by land and sea" after 1586, as she alleged in 1593, but was ready to resume it whenever the chance came'.

The last thing Fitzwilliam wanted, following on from the Armada, was any kind of repeat of the Desmond rebellion which, to no small extent, destroyed the reputation of his predecessor and which he knew could well tie down the military for months, even years, and infuriate the Queen because of its cost. His relationship with Bingham was now almost as acrimonious as Perrot's had been and, faced with the real possibility of a new and continuing revolt, he ordered him to stop all further action against the Bourkes. He then offered both them and their allies a truce, first suggesting Galway city as a meeting place (to which none of the participants would agree), then the small town of Newcastle outside.

It might be said here that had the Bourkes had any sense they would have grasped the olive branch and, in so doing, might have saved themselves a great deal of trouble and suffering, with the added possibility of actually having some influence on Bingham's subsequent career. But unfortunately they then started squabbling among themselves as to who should be the next MacWilliam, the main contender being Grace's brother-in-law William Bourke, the 'Blind Abbot', but his succession depended on the English agreeing to his doing so under the old Brehon law, not that set out and agreed in the Composition of Connaught. Their secondary demand, surely far more vital, was for the recall of Bingham for which there was considerable support even in London. It was the one ideal opportunity to have had him removed from the governorship of Connaught and they missed it.

The Queen also intervened personally, 'directing the Lord Deputy to adopt a more temperate course in the inferior governments, especially in Connaught'. On 7 June Fitzwilliam went into Athlone and arranged with the principal Bourke rebels (excepting the 'Devil's Hook') for them to submit and thus avoid any further fighting and bloodshed, and on 11 June they made their submission 'in St Nicholas Church, remaining on their knees almost three quarters of an hour'.

Having got that over, the next day they finally handed to Fitzwilliam their official list of complaints against Bingham, along with a petition asking by way of redress 'that a rate be laid down for pleading for pardons; that Bingham be removed from office; for a limit to be set on the extremity of martial law; that one of their number should be appointed to collect the Composition; that gentlemen of their own county be appointed as sheriffs in future; that no one should lose their lands or goods by provincial order without trial by law and that those who have been so disposed be restored; that part of the yearly profits of MacWilliam, allotted to the house of Castlebar and now in the Queen's hands, be given to William Bourke, the Blind Abbot, for his maintenance'.

The petition also detailed the many charges against

Bingham: his general contempt for the people, reflected in his administration of the province and the behaviour of his officials; his continual cruelty, including the murder of the unarmed and bound Owen O'Flaherty, his cavalier hanging of hostages, especially the elderly and infirm Edmund Bourke; the killings in Connaught in the wake of the Armada and his sending Browne into Mayo on the authority of an illegal commission to burn, pillage and kill.

After this, on 20 June a formal instrument was published setting out the terms and conditions for a peaceful settlement in exchange for full and complete apologies from all involved. The rebels listed, including Sir Morrough and William Bourke, 'the Blind Abbot, chief of the low Burkes', then put their names to the most cringing and abject series of apologies. At first, on reading it, it is hard to understand why they were prepared to be so comprehensively humiliated, when at the very least they had a good case against Bingham. Only later does one see what it was they had in mind. So, having provided Fitzwilliam with proof of their abject submission, the Bourkes and their allies departed, ensuring that this time they did not leave behind any family members as hostages.

Within no time it was obvious that the document to which they had put their names was not worth the paper it was written on. Almost immediately Grace and Tibbot sailed for Scotland with seven galleys in which to transport several hundred Redshanks, as Bingham immediately notified Walsingham, although later Grace refuted this. In October William Bourke, the Blind Abbot, was officially elected as the MacWilliam under the old Gaelic law in direct opposition to the English, after which the Bourkes recaptured Lough Mask Castle and set about raiding and plundering the country 'from Neale to Shrule'.

Faced again with such open insurrection, the Queen demanded that an end be put to it and that therefore the outstanding charges against Bingham, not all of which had by any means come from Connaught, should be resolved one way or another. The trial took place in Dublin: yet again he was acquitted. During the intervening time there had been a stand-off, but on 12 January a formal commission was given to Bingham to prosecute the rebels. After securing a number of hostages, on 1 February 1591 Bingham assembled a force of 890 soldiers and 228 kerne at Cong and then, accompanied by the Earls of Thomond and Clanricard, went into Mayo to take first of all Castlebar. Reporting to Walsingham, he wrote: 'The whole force which the Bourkes could make were not 900 men whereof the one half were churls, only armed with galloglas axes. We would have encountered 3000 of them such as they, for God knoweth they were most badly furnished, and very rags to look upon . . . If all the Irishry in Connaught were out in rebellion, both earls and others, they would not be able to make 3000 men to serve'. He then pointed out that 'the sons of Edmund Burke of Castlebarry are in the Low Countries . . .'

He pushed on, meeting only sporadic resistance, and on 8 February his forces reached Tirawley, unaware that they were being followed by a posse of Bourkes who felt themselves to have the advantage as Bingham had little or no cavalry with him. A number of Thomond's men, noticing a group of 'rebel kerne' crossing some nearby marshes on foot, set out after them unaware that they themselves were being followed by the horsemen who, seizing their opportunity, charged at them, killing two and wounding another. Bingham's report to Walsingham on what happened next is contained in the relevant State Papers headed by a note: 'Sir R. Bingham to Sir F. Walsyngham in answer to the letter of 17 March, received 18 April. Exculpates himself from blame in not writing oftener . . .' For it turned out that one of the horsemen was the Blind Abbot himself and that in the mêlée one of Thomond's men 'with his sword did strake him on the left leg and afterwards escaped away unhurt . . .' The sword slash was so severe that it almost severed the Blind Abbot's foot. His followers took their wounded chief over to an island in Lough Conn 'where a surgeon cut the foot off'.

Thus ended William Bourke's brief time as the MacWilliam. He was forced to give it up as the title carried with it the condition that its holder must be sound in wind and limb. Knox writes that he never rebelled again, accepted his pardon like the rest, 'and the last we hear of him is that he died in September 1598 in Thomond, and was buried in Quin Abbey'.

Bingham then continued on through Mayo to Clew Bay almost unimpeded, burning, looting and killing as he went. Many people simply took to the mountains, leaving everything behind including their cattle, at least 2,000 of which were rounded up and taken away by Bingham's men. When he reached Clew Bay, Bingham found that a considerable number of people had taken to their boats, making for the safety of Clare Island, Inisboffin and the other islands out in the bay. Baulked of his prey, as he had no boats, he contented himself with putting to the sword 'the churls, women and children' left behind. Faced with such an onslaught, the rebels, including the Clandonnel galloglas, began, a few at a time, to surrender although Tibbot and Edmund carried out a successful ambush of Bingham. It was beginning to look as if it would soon be over.

Bingham then turned his attention yet again to Grace who had escaped out to sea with her galleys. She was quite prepared to carry on the fight, so much so that when she heard that her second O'Flaherty son, Murrough, had not only submitted to the English, but had reached some kind of a deal with Bingham, she swore that she would teach him a lesson he would never forget.

Judging by the amount of correspondence from Bingham to various members of the Privy Council, he must have spent half his time sending in a constant stream of reports, possibly because he felt the need to ensure he got his side of the story in first. He informed William Cecil, Lord Burleigh, of the quarrel that had arisen between Grace and her son, writing that 'Mother Grany, being out of charity with her son for serving her Majesty, manned out her navy of galleys and landed in Ballinehencie where he dwelleth, burned his town and spoiled his people of their cattle and goods and murdered three or four of his men which offered to make resistance'. He was telling Burleigh this, he said, 'to give your Honour knowledge of her naughty disposition towards the State'.

Following what amounted to the end of the 'Blind Abbot rebellion', Bingham wrote yet another lengthy report to Walsingham in which he records: 'Immediately after the peace was concluded, Granye O'Maille, with two or three baggage boats full of knaves, not knowing that the peace was made committed some spoil in the Isles of Arran upon two or three of Sir Thomas Strange's men, to the value of twenty marks, which she did by persuasion of some of the O'Flaherteys presently, after Sir Thomas was dead. And indeed to the greatest cause of discontentment of challenge which Sir M [Murrough-ne-Doe O'Flaherty] had was losing these islands'. Richard Bourke must have been very concerned about what the consequences of his grandmother's actions might be, for Bingham adds a line saying that 'Richard Bourke, the Devil's Hook, hath Grana O'Malley in hand till she restore the spoils and repair the harms'.

This was to be the last letter Bingham would write to Walsingham. A note attached to it comments that 'this long and explanatory letter was written to Walsyngham (sic) before the news of his death had reached Sir Richard Bingham'. The Queen's spymaster, who had been fighting failing health for months, had finally given up the struggle. He had been one of her key advisers throughout her reign and would be greatly missed.

Then, unexpectedly, several hundred Redshanks arrived hoping to be employed by the Bourkes to fight the English, only to discover that it was almost all over, that there was nothing for them to do and that therefore they could not be paid. Enraged, they decided to help themselves and took whatever Bingham's men had left behind in the way of cattle and goods in north Mayo. The intrusion ended with the Redshanks fighting the very Bourkes they had come to assist, killing two of the Blind Abbot's sons and half-a-dozen of Grace's relations in the process. This was the one occasion when Grace, on being told the news and that the Scots were making for home, so far from 'drawing' them in, set off in hot pursuit.

Bingham duly reported to the Lord Deputy that two of the Blind Abbot's sons had been killed, along with two leaders of the Scots, and what a happy chance it was that they had set upon each other to the greater peace and tranquillity of the province. 'The Scots are now departed from hence towards their own country. And Grany O'Maly is preparing herself with some boats in her company to repair after them in revenge of her countrymen, and for the spoil they committed in these parts, which I am contented to tolerate, hoping that all or the most part will take their journey towards heaven, and the province be rid of many bad and ill-disposed persons.'

His wish was not granted and Grace returned home safely. But it was never to be the same again. Bingham now held all of Mayo and had cut the Bourke clans in half by setting up a garrison at Castlebar. A certain amount of sporadic activity continued during which an attempt by Tibbot to rescue a Clandonnell chieftain was successfully thwarted. But it was sufficient to turn Bingham's attention once again to the countryside around Clew Bay. Grace, returned from her voyaging, was once again settled in Rockfleet. Bingham had already taken almost all her cattle and horses, her source of land-based wealth, and he now took the rest. But this time he had another, and hitherto unused, weapon with which to subjugate her: English sea power. For the first time English fighting ships sailed into Clew Bay and proceeded to clean everyone and everything out of the islands, creeks and small ports which had been Grace's own territory for so long and from which she had operated as the Pirate Queen for forty years.

Almost her entire fleet was seized and, holed up as she was in Rockfleet, she could not have escaped even had she had a ship in which to do so. 'Our shipping,' wrote Bingham, jubilantly, to the Privy Council, 'has done great service for the same has cleared all their islands.' Grace had hit rock bottom. Like the Queen, she was now sixty years old, and she could be forgiven for thinking that the future held little or nothing for her, that there was nowhere else to go.

Indeed the outlook was exceedingly bleak. In September 1592 Tibbot submitted to Bingham at Ashnagower, agreeing that 'unto all things for the Bourkes, O'Malleys and Clangibbons be received into her Majesty's mercy and protection'. To be on the safe side Bingham insisted that his foster-father, Edmund MacTibbot, and a Macgibbon be handed over as hostages. To further weaken the clan structure, the system whereby vassal clans owed loyalty to their overall chieftain was abolished. From then on a chieftain was chief only of his own clan or sept, not of his vassals. Tibbot was also heavily fined for his part in the rebellion and had to make further restitution for any damage he had committed. A well-satisfied Bingham noted that Tibbot-ne-Long and his half-brother, Edmund, were now 'men of no possessions', left without so much as half-a-dozen cows apiece.

Civil servants, pedantic as ever, carefully recorded the cost of the Bourke rebellions, not in human life and suffering, but in hard cash:

War against Bourkes and Scots in 1586: £1,476 3s. 4d.
War against Bourkes, Scots and others 1589–1590 £3296 17s. 6d.

Note that it was estimated down to the exact shillings and pence.

13

Talking to the Queen

Bingham might have been exaggerating when he bragged that he had reduced Tibbot and Edmund to such beggary that they no longer had so much as half-a-dozen cows apiece, but he was not far wide of the mark. The rebellions, and his brutal suppression of them, had to all intents and purposes bankrupted the Bourkes and reduced the population of Mayo to a bare subsistence level. As for Grace, she was now fighting for her very survival, a battle which would result in her famous visit to London when she was granted a personal audience with Queen Elizabeth.

This is where the dichotomy in respect of Grace and her place in the history of the times is at its most marked. On the one hand there is the high romanticised legend made so much of today in which the event is billed as 'the meeting of the two Queens', and where Grace, by her bearing and courage, triumphs over Elizabeth. On the other hand – which would explain her neglect by Irish historians for so long – is a deep-seated suspicion that by this action, above all others, she betrayed her own people and possibly could never have been trusted. Given the complexity of the politics and the shifting of loyalties in Mayo throughout the sixteenth century (described by one historian as being worse than in any other county), it is likely that the truth lies somewhere between the two.

First and foremost on Grace's agenda had always been the survival of herself and her immediate family, especially Tibbot, even though on a number of occasions her actions can only be described as rash; as we have seen, when sufficiently enraged, even *family* loyalty went by the board and she could turn on her own son. But when it comes to considering Grace and her actions, rarely is anything simple. Now she realised that unless she took some drastic action, one way or another Bingham would get her in the end, and this time there would be no last-minute reprieve on the scaffold. If any further spur were needed, in May 1593 Tibbot was imprisoned in Athlone Castle, charged by Bingham with treason. The incident which led to it had taken place during what would be seen later as the first stirrings of yet another rebellion, one that would lead in turn to the Nine Years War.

For a truly major player had now come on the scene, Hugh O'Neill, Earl of Tyrone, handsome, charismatic, subtle, very clever – and English-educated. He really knew his enemy. He looked at what had been happening in Ireland during the last ten years and didn't like what he saw. Munster, following the ending of the Desmond rebellion, had been laid waste, Connaught reduced to penury. In each case lands and goods belonging to rebels had been handed over to English incomers. There was little doubt in Tyrone's mind that Ulster would be next. Therefore, while presenting every appearance of complete loyalty to the Crown, he was in fact in contact with another Hugh, 'Red Hugh O'Donnell', who shared both his fears and his determination to do something about matters.

As if that was not complicated enough, yet another Hugh, the dashing Hugh Maguire, had raided Sligo and Roscommon at the head of some thousand men after Bingham had 'proclaimed' county Monaghan and hanged the chief of the MacMahons. In retaliation, Maguire burned down the town of Ballymote, which was under the control of Bingham's brother, George. During the skirmish that followed, several of Maguire's men were captured by Bingham and one of them, quite possibly to save his own skin, claimed that Tibbot had been involved. Tibbot's alleged crime was that he had written a letter in Irish to one, Brian O'Rourke, offering to 'make stirs' and that if he, O'Rourke, could hold out for another two months Tibbot would undertake that, as Bingham put it, 'the banished rebel, the Devil's Hook, and the rest should return to Mayo again and with his help make war'. Which begs the questions, when was the Devil's Hook, 'and the rest', banished, where to, and why? But Bingham did not stop at Tibbot; for good measure, he also took into custody Grace's half-brother, the peaceable 'Donal of the Pipes', and charged him with murder.

Fearful for their lives, for she was all too aware given his past reputation that Bingham would be quite capable of hanging them first and justifying his actions later, Grace realised her only hope was to seek another pardon, this time directly from the Queen herself. Also, given her treatment at Bingham's hands, she would attempt to obtain the restitution of at least some of her rights, though she must have realised this would be no easy matter given her past history of ignoring her own submissions as well as the pardon she had been granted in Dublin. As to influence, if she had ever had a relationship with Walsingham based on providing him from time to time with intelligence, then his death had brought that to an end. His place as Secretary of State to the Privy Council and chief spymaster had been taken in an 'acting' capacity by Burleigh's ambitious son, Robert Cecil, a man destined to go down in history as a real Machiavellian. For whatever reason, possibly simple dislike, it took Elizabeth seven years to confirm Cecil in the appointment he had craved for so long, during which time he did the work required without payment from her and at his own expense.

Grace began, therefore, with breathtaking nerve by contacting the other great political survivor of the Elizabethan Court, Cecil's father Burleigh. Her letter is in the form of a petition, and the published edition of the relevant State Papers is in English, although the original must almost certainly have been in Latin. It is interesting because, after the accepted flowery opening, she gets down to the business of giving the Queen her own version of recent events in Connaught, along with a brief autobiographical profile and her strong views on the rough treatment handed out to widows in Ireland.

First of all she explains why she became involved in the recent rebellion. It was because of 'the continued discord, stirs and dissensions which heretofore long time remained among the Irish, especially in West Connaught by the sea side, every chieftain for his safeguard and maintenance and for the defence of his people, followers and country took arms by strong hand to make head against his neighbours, who in like manner constrained your highness fond subject to take arms and by force to maintain herself by sea and land the space of forty years past'. There we have it in a nutshell. For forty years she had been forced solely by events not of her own making to take up piracy as her only means of making a living and then to take part in the recent rebellion. Otherwise, she implies, she would have remained happily at home with her spinning wheel, looking after her various households.

She gives the Queen a brief history of her two marriages, explains that widows in Ireland have no rights to any of their late husbands' land or property, and asks therefore that the Queen might give her some form of an allowance from the rents and taxes collected by the Crown from their estates, a request she makes 'in tender consideration whereof and in regard of her great age, she most humbly beseeches your Majesty of your princely bounty and liberality to grant her some reasonable maintenance for the little time she has to live'. She further asks the Queen to accept the submission of her sons, Tibbot-ne-Long and Murrough O'Flaherty, so that they may hold their lands and rents again, a request she also makes on behalf of two of her Bourke relations, another Walter Bourke and Shane Burke MacWilliam. She ends by pleading with the Queen 'under her signet, free liberty during her life' to take on and fight 'with sword and fire all your Highness' enemies, wheresoever they are or shall be, without any interruption of any person or persons whatsoever'.

This latter can only be a reference to Bingham. It may well be that her unsolicited offer to take on any of Elizabeth's future enemies in person is what later damned her in the eyes of many. The petition was duly despatched, and it would be interesting to know exactly how and why it not only reached the Queen so quickly but was also attended to with such speed. Petitions flooded into Elizabeth in a ceaseless tide, some waiting weeks, months or even years before they received an answer. Some were never seen at all. Yet here, as it must have been viewed by those at Court, the elderly widow of two obscure Irish chieftains, a woman who had been a thorn in the flesh of the governor of Connaught for years, who had twice been imprisoned and once nearly executed, let alone having been closely involved in a recent rebellion, was apparently having her petition expedited. There is no clue as to who undertook the task, though later correspondence was said to have reached Elizabeth through the offices of the Earl of Ormond. But however it happened, it caught the interest of the Queen.

It is difficult to chart the exact sequence of subsequent events, but she must have been in London by the time the famous eighteen 'Articles of Interrogatory' were put to her by Burleigh, for in them there is a mention of Sir

Murrough-ne-Doe Flaherty, 'presently at Court', and he must have sailed with her from Ireland. All eighteen questions had to be fully answered if she was to stand any chance of an audience with the Queen. However, there is no argument that at some time towards the end of June she sailed up the Thames, legend has it captaining her own ship. With her as well as Sir Murrough-ne-Doe, who had a petition of his own to address to Her Majesty concerning the actions of Bingham, were the sons of Ulick Bourke of Erris and Tibbot Reagh Bourke, 'attending on Grany O'Maille' while she was at Court. She seems to have brought something of an entourage with her.

It was at this juncture that Bingham woke up and realised what was happening. In a frantic letter to Burleigh (in which his spelling in the original becomes more creative with every line), he warns him that 'there be two notable traitors gone over, Sir Morrough-Ne Doe and Grainy O'Maly both rebels from their childhood and continually in action and if such be heard to complain against the officer or rewarded with anything from her Majesty it will be the highway to make more rebels: but they may challenge their reward to be in Byrdwell [Bridewell Prison], for notwithstanding that they have many pardons, there is matter enough of late found out against them to hang them by justice. Grany O'Maly is mother-in-law to the notable traitor, the Devil's Hook. Howbeit (my most honourable good Lord) let them directly accuse me of anything, and if I discharge not myself honestly I am to be punished for it; but if they be drawn on to make general exclamations against me I do not doubt but your Honour will most Honourably and indifferently consider it, for if they belie me not, I care not what all of them say against me'.

Which one might describe as getting one's retribution in first. There is no doubt that Bingham was thoroughly alarmed at the possible consequences of allowing Grace and Sir Murrough free rein to publicise what had gone on in Connaught. Grace's first task was to respond to Burleigh's eighteen questions. (See Appendix.) The questions covered her ancestry, information about her parents, her first husband, the children she had had by him and their names and whereabouts, what 'countries' (presumably lands) they had on which to maintain themselves, and the names of their spouses. 'What kin,' asked Burleigh, 'was O'Flaherty her first husband to Sir Murrough 'Ne Dough O'Flaherty who is here now at the Court?'

She had then to answer similar questions about her second husband and any children of that marriage, and her stepsons. Most important to Grace was that she was asked if she had been allowed her dower, or thirds of her husbands' livings (as might have been the case in England) and if not, what amount would she have needed to maintain herself after her last husband's death? A tricky one, that. What was the relationship between the two young men she had brought with her to her son, Tibbot? What 'captains and countries' lay next to the O'Flaherty possessions and who owned the 'House of Moriske upon the seaside in Owle O'Maly. What lands does McGibbon possess in Mayo and who owns the lands named Carramore and Mayn Connell, the Island of Achill and 'Kill' Castle? What kin was her last husband to Walter and Ulick Bourke?'

The Irish love tracing their genealogy and Grace was no exception, so she answered the first two questions very fully, but the third at even greater length. The expected answer would have taken up only a couple of lines, but she used it as an opportunity to launch an all-out attack on Bingham, his activities in Mayo and the murder of her son, Owen. She was then asked what financial provision was made for the widows of Irish gentry on their husbands' deaths and if the Composition of Connaught had addressed the issue. She seems to have been under the impression that English widows were entitled to a third of their husbands' estate and told Burleigh that 'the Irishry' had never yielded any 'thirds' to a woman surviving a chieftain, only the value of her dowry, and that the Composition of Connaught had merely confirmed this, 'wherein no mention is made of any such', and so had done nothing 'to relieve the wife of any chieftain after his death'. In her answer to the tenth question she elaborated on her grievance over the fate of Irish widows at greater length, recording her own experiences, before giving brief responses to the remaining queries.

The meeting between Grace and Elizabeth is likely to have taken place towards the end of July when the Queen was at one of her summer palaces, most likely Nonsuch or Richmond. Grace had not chosen a good time for the visit, for 1593 was a truly terrible Plague year. King Pest stalked the streets of London and brightness, as the poet Nashe wrote, 'falls from the air'. As a result the Court and most of the nobility had left the city for the suburbs and countryside. As well as further Armada scares from time to time, there was trouble back home in London, for during 1592 and 1593 there had been a major influx of refugees escaping religious persecution on the Continent, particularly from the Low Countries.

As the numbers of Plague cases grew, so also did the rumours that it was being brought into the country and spread by those we would call asylum seekers today. Unpleasant notices were flyposted in public places, racist graffiti appeared on walls. There were attacks on foreigners, and apprentices roamed the warrens and alleyways of the Bankside looking for trouble. To give it its due the Privy Council acted with exemplary haste, issuing an Order to the effect that the publishing of such 'malicious libels' should end forthwith and that anyone so doing would be punished with the utmost severity. Officers of the law, therefore, would now have the right to search home or workplace or lodgings to hunt such persons down. If caught, they would be arrested and if they refused to confess their guilt, 'you shall have authority, therefore,' the Order continues, 'to put them to the torture in Bridewell . . . and draw from them such knowledge that they have'. But such an Order gave the authorities *carte blanche* to look for those suspected of other misdemeanours, which is how the dramatist Thomas Kyd came to be arrested and tortured in order to incriminate the far more famous and dangerous Christopher Marlowe. Marlowe met his end in Deptford on 30 May 1593 after meeting up with none other than Mary Stewart's betrayer, Robert Poley.

So the London that Grace came to was in the grip of various fears: of a further attack by Spain; of an infection which could attack you in the morning and kill you before midnight; of the strangers from the Continent and what they might bring with them; and, not least, of Cecil's men who could burst into your house at any time of the day or night and drag you off to Bridewell where the rack awaited those who did not freely confess or, like poor Kyd, did not even know what it was they were supposed to have done. Perhaps it should be noted that Bingham specified Bridewell (the only prison outside the Tower with a rack) as a suitable place to incarcerate Grace and Sir Murrough, rather than the better-known Newgate.

This, then, was the background to the meeting of the two women who, whether they realised it or not, had reached a similar point in both their lives. Elizabeth's reign reached its apogee with the great speech at Tilbury in 1588 when she had been faced with the might of Spain. Had there been speech writers in those days it might well now be attributed to Shakespeare, but Elizabeth herself was no mean hand at the use of glorious language. That was Elizabeth Regina in her full majesty, the great and splendid icon who had given England years of peace and was now prepared like Henry V to lead her troops into battle. The woman who had survived appalling dangers in childhood and adolescence, who had found herself in the Tower accused of treason while still in her teens, would go down in history as one of the greatest English monarchs of all time.

But for Elizabeth too, like Grace, the glory days were over. It would not be until her deathbed that she would finally confirm James VI of Scotland as her successor and James I of England, but already the traffic between London and Edinburgh was growing steadily, a path increasingly beaten by young sprigs of nobility on the make, influential older men busy sounding out the situation, spies (of course) and an increasing number of Cecil's own confidential messengers. Cecil saw as his great mission the peaceful and uncontested handover of power to James when the time came. Ironically, Mary Stewart had triumphed in death. So the woman who faced Grace across the audience room was now sixty years old, the once abundant red hair thin, grey and always hidden under a wig, her face a rigid mask of make-up framed by an enormous lace rough, her teeth rotten, and when dressed for such an occasion hardly able to move for the weight of her jewels and the heavy, brocaded gown stretched over an enormous farthingale.

As for Grace, her almost total command of the seaboard of the west coast of Ireland (Bingham reckoned that at one time she had as many as twenty vessels in her fleet) was also a thing of the past. About the same age as Elizabeth and with so much of her life spent at sea, her appearance must have been striking in a very different way, for it is unlikely that she would have hidden her weatherbeaten face behind make-up. As to dress, no doubt

she wore her very best ('thinking herself no small lady
. . .') but it would hardly have matched up to the fashion
and sophistication of the wives of noblemen at the
English Court, let alone the Queen. This never was a
meeting of 'two queens', but in their different ways their
hard, hazardous and dangerous lives had given them at
least one thing in common: the ability to survive.

To start then with the fairytale version of what
happened, the one set out in the Rev. Caesar Otway's 1839
account in his book, *A Tour of Connaught*, which is based
largely on what he was told, further laced with his own
imaginings and written in convoluted style: 'Grana,
having made her bow, and held out her bony hand, horny
as it was with many an oar she had handled and many
a helm she had held, to her sister Elizabeth (as she called
her), sat down with as much self-possession and self-
respect as an American Indian chief would now before
the President of the United States.

'Elizabeth, observing Grana's fondness for snuff,
which though a practice newly introduced, she had
picked up in her smuggling enterprises, and, perceiving
her inconvenienced as snuffers usually are when want-
ing a pocket handkerchief, presented her with one richly
embroidered, which Grana took indifferently, used
loudly, and cast away carelessly: and when asked by Sir
Walter Raleigh why she had treated the gift of her
Majesty in such a way, the answer of that wild Irish girl
(sic) was of that coarseness which ought not to be read
by ears polite.'

Moreover, he continued, she did not seem happy with
the present the Queen offered to her, a lapdog 'led in a
silken band'. 'What's this for', says Grana. 'Oh, it's a saga-
cious, playful and faithful little creature, it will lie in
your lap.' 'My lap!', says Grana, 'it's little the likes of me
would be doing with such a thing – keep it yourself,
Queen of the English, it is only fit for idlers such as you;

you may, if it likes you, fool away your day with such vermin.' 'Oh but,' says Elizabeth, 'Grana, you are mistaken. I have the care of this great country on my shoulders.' 'Maybe so', says Grana, 'but as far as I can see of your ways, there's many a poor creature in Mayo, who has only the care of a barley field, has more industry about them than you seem to have.'

'Of course Elizabeth dismissed her soon – she offered at her last audience to create her a countess. "I don't want your titles," says Grana. "Aren't we both equals? If there be any good in the thing in it I might as well make you one as you me. Queen of England, I want nothing from you – enough for me is it to be head of my nation, but you may do what you like with my little son, Toby of the Ship, who has Saxon blood in his veins, and may not be dishonoured by a Saxon title. I will remain as I am: Grane O'Maille of the Uisles."'

It is, of course, pure fantasy. We have no official account of what took place when the two women met, probably once, possibly twice, but the myth could hardly be further from the truth. Elizabeth would have been surrounded by her ladies and would have had, one imagines, at least one adviser with her (quite possibly Burleigh himself), and rumours of such gross insolence would soon have got about. Indeed the Queen might well have acted on Bingham's suggestion and had Grace removed at once to Bridewell. On her part Grace must have been aware of the considerable privilege afforded to her: she was only the second Irish rebel to whom the Queen had granted such a personal audience, the first being Shane O'Neill. It is understood that the conversation was conducted in Latin and it is disappointing that no record was kept of it or that, if it was, it no longer exists.

As to her general attitude, Grace may well have been used to command, but first and foremost she was pleading for the lives of herself, her son and her half-brother, and for her right to live without being in constant fear of imprisonment or worse. She had also been brought to the brink of abject poverty, her property seized, her cattle and horses taken by Bingham, her fleet impounded, and she was asking that a proportion of the income from the rents and taxes paid to the Crown from the land of both husbands be allocated to her for her maintenance. Nor was she stupid. This was no time for a show of arrogance. Nor is it remotely possible that she would ever have claimed to be the 'head of her nation'. What nation? A country of tribes always fighting each other when they were not fighting the English? Men prepared to turn on their closest family members and murder them to be 'head' of a mere sept of a clan, let alone 'head' of a country?

Also, as Elizabeth was constantly being asked to grant audiences and time was precious, she would not have been prepared to waste it talking of dogs and handkerchiefs. Presumably she had been briefed by Burleigh as to Grace's background and career and quite possibly had read her replies to Burleigh's questions. There would have been much to discuss: Grace's past reneging on submissions and a pardon, her promise now of loyalty to the Crown, the fate of her son and half-brother, how she proposed to conduct herself when she returned home, what she might need in the way of maintenance. Possibly even services rendered to Walsingham in the past. But there is no doubt that she impressed Elizabeth and convinced her that this time she meant what she said.

Grace remained in and 'around the Court' until September waiting to hear the result of her plea. London must have been a culture shock: the houses of the nobles and rich merchants, the teeming wharves and the sheer number of people. If she was tempted to indulge her taste for gambling, then there were plenty of gambling dens on the Bankside looking for country folk to gull if she was willing to take the risk; if she did, then no doubt she would have been well able to hold her own. But the times were abnormal, the theatres and playhouses closed most of the time because of the Plague, and public gatherings of most other kinds banned. If she was indeed about the Court, then she is likely to have remained for most of the time well outside Westminster and the City.

So far from acting on Bingham's advice, after she had spoken with Grace the Queen told the Privy Council to ask him why he was holding Tibbot, Donal and (wrongly as it happened) Grace's son Morough prisoner. Also for an explanation of his conduct towards Grace and her family and the killing of Owen O'Flaherty. To add insult to injury Bingham was also asked how best Grace could be provided with an income to maintain her. This time Bingham was shaken to the core. All kinds of unpleasant possibilities were being opened up and he decided that the best form of defence was attack. He wanted to know where the information in the letter sent to him had come from and, with breathtaking hypocrisy, demanded that the complainant 'show me one instance of any one that ever I used violence against, having always (I thank the Lord) had that consideration of Christian duty as I never sought any man's blood otherwise than in the course of her [Majesty's] common laws to take away'.

Not only that, but Grace and others had had ample opportunity, while making 'stirs' in the state, to make such complaints against him, yet they had not done so. Now, however, 'they [Grace and Sir Murrough] are pulled down and forced in spite of their hearts to submit themselves to her Majesty's laws, they pretend many wrongs and are not ashamed to ask for recompense'. As for giving Grace maintenance, he'd give her maintenance! He would ask 'for a boat of some thirty tons with which to beat her, with God's assistance, and drive her and all her fleet into the sea'.

There followed an uneasy hiatus for some weeks, during which Grace continued to fear for the lives of Tibbot and Donal. However, on 6 September the Queen sent an answer to Bingham (a copy of which exists in the Cecil Papers). She noted that Bingham had denied that he was holding Murrough O'Flaherty prisoner and that he posed no threat of any kind; indeed, 'as a dutiful subject hath served us when his mother, being accompanied with a number of disorderly person, did with her "galleys" spoil him'. As to Tibbot, allegedly accused of sending a treasonable letter to Brian O'Rourke, and Donal, imprisoned now some seven months, accused of 'having been in the company of certain men that killed some soldiers in a ward', they should both be released at once 'upon bonds for their good behaviour, wherein we are content'.

Regarding Grace, 'we are content', the Queen wrote, 'so as the old woman may understand we yield thereto in regard of her humble suit; so she is hereof informed and departeth with great thankfulness and with many most earnest promises that she will, as long as she lives, continue a dutiful subject, yea, and will employ all her power to offend and prosecute any offender against us'. And as to her plea for financial assistance: 'further for the pity to be had of this aged woman, having not by the custom of the Irish any title to any livelihood or portion of her two husbands' lands, now being a widow and yet her sons enjoying their fathers' lands, we require you to deal with her sons in our name and to yield to her some maintenance...', the amount to be decided, then deducted from the sums they paid to the Crown. She trusted that Bingham 'shall with your favour in all their good causes protect them to live in peace to enjoy their livelihoods'.

Grace sailed again for Ireland towards the end of September, taking with her a copy of the Queen's letter which she delivered in person to Bingham before taking up residence once again in Rockfleet. For weeks he did all he could to avoid obeying the Queen's commands, to the point where in November Grace confronted him, swearing that if he did not do as he was told she would set out again for London to inform the Queen herself. Finally, and with great reluctance, Bingham released both Tibbot and Donal, Tibbot having been so badly treated that he could hardly stand. Grace appeared to have won game, set and match against Bingham and, furnished with the Queen's permission to fight her enemies on her behalf, she set about acquiring three new galleys which, it was said, could hold three hundred men at a time.

14

The O'Neill – War in Ulster

Grace's undoubted triumph in achieving such a positive outcome to her meeting with the Queen should have allowed her to live out the rest of her natural life in comparative comfort from the maintenance she was to receive from her former husbands' estates. It also allowed her to add some kind of respectability to her activities along the western seaboard so long as what she did could loosely be described as taking action against the Queen's enemies.

But it was not to be, not only because of Bingham's continuing obsessive animosity towards her but also because, overshadowing that was the uprising in Ulster led by Hugh O'Neill, described as the most dangerous of the whole of Elizabeth's reign, which was to turn into the Nine Years War. Expensive both in terms of cost and human life, not to mention the humiliation of the English at the Battle of Yellow Ford, it finally ended with English victory at Kinsale and the subsequent 'Flight of the Wild Geese', the desperate escape of O'Neill and the other leaders of the rebellion to exile in Spain. Its most spectacular English victim was Elizabeth's last great favourite, Robert Devereux, Earl of Essex.

We left Grace at the end of the last chapter energetically fitting out her three new galleys ready to resume her activities, but Bingham was having none of it. So far as he was concerned, whatever she might have promised the Queen of England and received in return, it cut no ice with him. He therefore detailed a Captain Straites and a troop of soldiers to monitor her every move and accompany her on all her voyages, presumably by boat, although this is not specified. Their actions forced her, as she wrote later, to 'repair to the seas' and to the islands where some eighteen Bourkes, who had been proclaimed traitors, 'were killed'. The slaughtered Bourkes were the remnants of the rag-tag army assembled by the Devil's Hook's son, Richard Bourke, in support of Hugh Maguire.

Knox describes what happened. A Captain Clarke with two bands of Irish soldiers raised by the Governor (Bingham), but 'officered and commanded by Englishmen', was sent after them and pursued them in boats among the islands. He surprised the rebels in Inishkea (an island off the Achill Peninsula). 'About 120 in all, of whom eighty were able men, Richard (son of the Devil's Hook) and some half a dozen escaped in a boat. The rest, finding escape impossible, stood manfully to it. All were killed or drowned. Captain Clarke lost but three or four killed and four wounded. Before this action had finished . . . Tibbot na Long had been released and had gone to help in hunting down his rebellious kinsmen. Some thirty heads of rebel Bourkes and their followers were sent to the Governor at Cloonagashel. All was over by mid-November.' One can only imagine the grisly scene when the thirty heads were presented to Bingham.

Nor had Bingham made any attempt to arrange for Grace to receive the maintenance to which the Queen had agreed she was entitled. Worse, in spite of Tibbot actually being prepared to turn against his own family and assist the English, and indirectly Bingham, in the slaughter of his own kinsmen on Inishkea (an action which remains contentious even today), he was determined to impoverish Grace and her family even further. He forced her to give quarters to a troop of his own men for seven months, during which time they were encouraged to eat and drink as much as they liked. Whether or not it was what he had in mind, his actions eventually drove Grace, Tibbot and a small band of her followers out of Mayo, sailing in one of her galleys to seek refuge with Thomas ('Black Tom'), Earl of Ormond, in Munster.

Grace had found the Earl to be sympathetic to her when she visited London, and his support now would give her a very real advantage. From his earliest days at the English Court, Ormond had been on good terms with the Queen, so good that at one time there was gossip that he had supplanted even Robert Dudley in her favour. Indeed a Spanish Ambassador had reported back to King Philip that Ormond had been reproved by the Archbishop of York for his relationship with Elizabeth. It is highly unlikely that the rumours were true, but most commentators on the period agree that there was a sentimental link between the two, a real friendship, stronger than that which might be expected to bind a Queen and subject, and that subject a man of 'exceptional personal charm'.

Ormond, who intensely disliked Bingham, welcomed the fugitives to his manor at Carrick, and on 17 April 1595 he wrote a covering letter to the Privy Council on her behalf, to accompany a further petition to the Queen even though, he writes, he was somewhat loath to do so at the present time, 'considering . . . the weighty causes which now troubled them'. He also states that Grace is the 'bearer' of her petition, which lends some weight to the suggestion that she returned to London in May 1595 to put her case in person, if not to the Queen, then to a person of importance, although if she did there is no further record of it and the phrase she uses, 'at my last being here', could as well refer to her previous visit.

In her petition Grace reminded the Queen of their meeting two years earlier and the agreement made between them in which she had promised to continue 'a dutiful subject' to her Majesty, along with her sons, cousins and followers. On her return she had fitted out three galleys to seek out the Queen's enemies but had been thwarted by Bingham's surveillance of her every move and his attempt to force her on to the islands where the Bourkes, proclaimed as traitors, had taken refuge. Then, on land, Bingham had quartered his men on her to the point of impoverishment, 'contrary to the covenants promised on your Majesty's behalf in discharge whereof your supplicant and the rest with all the inhabitants of Connaught have yielded to pay . . . that yearly rent by the name of Composition rent'.

She promised that she and her family 'with a hundred men at their own charge at sea along the coast of Ireland' would serve the Queen in her Majesty's wars upon all occasions every year from Easter until Michaelmas and asked that the Queen accept the surrender of her sons and cousins and all their manors, castles, islands, towns, lands and hereditaments in Connaught, to be held in future from the Queen and her heirs and successors, and to grant her gracious letters to the Lord Deputy of Ireland upon acceptance of that surrender. In exchange for which they should be allowed to take up their patrimonies and inheritance, paying the rents and duties agreed and confirmed on her Majesty's behalf. More to the point, her family would, from then on, 'put their lives at all times in danger to the advancement of her highness' service but also pray for your honourable lordships' success long to live in happiness'. The latter sentence suggests that the Petition was aimed at the Privy Council in general rather than a particular member.

Having received no swift reply, on 5 May Grace wrote again asking for pardon for her 'boldness', asking that at the very least she might be allowed to live out the rest of her life without the constant fear of being put to death by some means or other either by Bingham or one of his cohorts, 'which hath been attempted sundry times'. She also pointed out that two years after her original petition she had still not been granted the third parts of the lands and rents of her O'Flaherty and Bourke husbands.

While she may not have received a swift reply, it is almost certain that the Privy Council, and in particular Burleigh, would have given her petition their attention. What she was now offering in the way of loyalty and assistance on behalf of herself and her family might well prove extremely valuable when it came to fighting O'Neill, and the Council had already received some proof of that, for in April Tibbot had also written to them (in English) listing the names of the Bourkes he had personally killed at Inishkea as evidence of his loyalty. To set against this was the history of the wavering allegiance of both of them, and the disregard of earlier solemn promises, but the Privy Council was under no illusion: it would need all the help it could get. It was the quiet before the storm. There was no doubt that Hugh O'Neill and his ally, 'Red' Hugh O'Donnell, were preparing for all-out war against the English and would be looking for assistance from as many of the major clans as possible, including the O'Malleys and Bourkes of Mayo. In spite of the repression following, first, the Desmond rebellion, then the Armada, there was no guarantee that eventually the whole country would rise and join O'Neill.

In 1594 there had been yet another change of Lord Deputy, Sir William Russell, son of the Earl of Bedford, replacing Sir William Fitzwilliam who had been recalled. Taking advantage of his inexperience, Hugh O'Neill had promptly made humble submission to him, promised to restore peace in Ulster, get rid of the Scots, pay his Composition rents and send his eldest son to England to be educated either at Oxford or Cambridge and serve as hostage for his good behaviour. Russell had gone along with all this and had now incurred the wrath of the Queen for his 'foul oversight'. By May 1597 he too had been replaced: by Sir Thomas Burgh, who reported that English rule and authority was now non-existent in the north and that while O'Neill's promise still held, it would be only a matter of time before he broke it. In the Pale he could not decide, one observer comments, which was more grievous, the outcries of the soldiers for want of pay, or of the country people whom they had robbed and pillaged.

The Anglican Bishop of Cork wrote to Lord Hunsdon at that time: 'Our State here is very dangerous. Five J.P.'s sit on the Bench every sessions, yet never took Oath of Supremacy to her Majesty. Two refused point blank. Whereas in England I might have had a thousand or more in church at sermon, I now have not five, and whereas I had five hundred communicants or more, now there are not three in spite of providing the populace with Bibles, New Testaments, and Communion Books in both English and Latin ... But none will come to church at all, not so much as the country churls; they follow their seducers, the priests'.

There is no record that Grace ever received a response either to her second petition or the letter that followed, but while never taking any part in the main action, it was impossible for her and her family not to become involved to some extent in what was to come. Finally O'Neill and O'Connell threw caution to the winds and directly petitioned the King of Spain for help. It seems they had real problems in persuading sufficient galloglas to fight on their behalf, although they had been promised supplies of powder and shot from Glasgow. One reason for this might be that on the death of his English wife Mabel, née Bagenal, Hugh O'Neill had married Catherine Magennis, the daughter of Lord Iveagh, returning to the Macdonalds the young woman of their family (and presumed future bride) who had been brought over from Scotland for his approval. O'Neill therefore asked the King for two to three thousand men with money and arms for their own. By so doing 'we hope', he wrote, 'to restore the faith of the Church and so secure you a kingdom'. He signed it with the proscribed title of 'the O'Neill' and sealed it with the sign of the Red Hand of Ulster.

While Sir Richard Bingham might have been the most notorious member of the family, nepotism had seen to the advancement in Ireland of both his brothers, George and John, and, more recently, of his cousin, Captain George Bingham. In June 1595 Captain Bingham was murdered by a Bourke member of his own troop of soldiers, Ulick Bourke, who then 'betrayed' the town of Newry to O'Donnell who took it over, knowing that Bingham had insufficient means at his disposal to retake it. It also gave O'Donnell control of the town of Ballyshannon, an important crossing point on the Erne River with access to Sligo, which was strategically very important. Without more ado O'Donnell captured Sligo Castle which gave him immediate and unimpeded access into Mayo. While this might have made strategic sense, it was not the best way of ensuring the support of the Mayo clans. The O'Donnells had a traditional claim, hotly contested by the Bourkes, to be overlords of North Mayo and from the start took great exception to what they saw as little better than an invasion. But instead of making every effort to bring the O'Malleys and the Bourkes on side, O'Donnell treated Mayo as if it were enemy territory, allowing his men to loot and plunder at will anything not already seized by Bingham. The unfortunate inhabitants were caught between a rock and a hard place: Bingham on the one side and O'Donnell on the other, with little or nothing to choose between them.

In the run-up to the war proper, there followed a period which can only be described as one of muddle and confusion. Minor chieftains in the north swore loyalty and submitted to the Crown but with, as Falls dryly puts it, 'no sincerity on the Irish side in these dealings and at best a vague hope that something favourable would turn up on the English'. Meanwhile back home, the English were frantically trying to raise levies of troops from Northumberland and Lancashire in the north, through the midland counties as far south as Oxfordshire and east to Leicestershire, down to Devon in the west as Hugh O'Neill, Earl of Tyrone, was proclaimed a traitor. But as fast as they recruited men, so those already in place were either taken ill, or deserted, or both. Meanwhile the War Treasurer, Sir Henry Wallop, was spelling out to Burleigh what the cost of it was likely to be and that all these levied men would have to be fed. There was beef and malt in Ireland, but meal, biscuit, wheat and some cheese would have to be sent from England and money would be needed to salt meat and herring for the garrisons of Armagh and Monaghan.

For some time O'Neill had been receiving encouragement from Spain, and early in 1596 he was promised that help would come within the year and, true to their word, the Spaniards began fitting out a fleet to go to his relief. Unfortunately, however, England got wind of it and in June Lord Howard, in command of a fleet carrying 6,000 soldiers under the command of the Earl of Essex, descended on Cadiz. In the harbour were between fifteen and twenty galleys and over forty merchantmen. Instead of seeing to these first, Essex landed his troops and assaulted the city, which surrendered to him after bitter street fighting. A ransom was paid for the lives of the inhabitants, whereupon Essex let loose his men and Cadiz was looted. He hailed it on his return as a great triumph, but in actual fact he had managed things so ineptly that half the galleys got away unscathed and the merchantmen were able to unload and hide much of their cargo. However, the Cadiz raid proved to be a very real setback for O'Neill's hopes of urgent help from Spain. A further attempt to send a fleet, 'the Second Armada', to Ireland in October 1597 ran into weather similar to that of its predecessor in 1588, the ships were scattered, and Spain suffered heavy losses in both vessels and men.

Throughout this time O'Donnell had been consolidating himself in Mayo, compelling the Mayo chieftains by force of arms to go along with him, and it would seem that in spite of everything they had sworn and said, Grace, Tibbot and the rest of the Bourkes had no option but to follow suit, or so they claimed. However, in July 1596 Grace's prayers were finally answered: Sir Richard Bingham was removed from the scene. Bingham's enemies in England and Ireland had been making a case against him for some time and they had finally succeeded in persuading Sir William Russell that much of the trouble throughout Connaught arose from his continuing severity. At first Russell was reluctant to act but eventually the animosity to Bingham was such that he suspended him while making further enquiries into his conduct. But Bingham, left to kick his heels in Dublin and infuriated by his treatment, jumped the gun and left for England in September without seeking the Lord Deputy's permission. He went straight to London, where he was promptly incarcerated in the Fleet Prison on charges of oppression and extortion.

After some delay a new Governor of Connaught, Sir Conyers Clifford, was appointed in his place with a brief to build bridges and encourage the Mayo chiefs to back the Crown. Clifford, though a professional soldier, was a very different kind of man to Bingham. Within a short time he had received the submission of several of the Connaught chiefs who had given their reluctant allegiance to O'Donnell, among them Tibbot whom Clifford saw as a useful future ally. Tibbot's half-brother, Edmund, had recently been killed in Galway, after which Tibbot had emerged as the likely leader of the Mayo clans. He also had added personal reasons for turning on O'Donnell, for yet again the question of who should be the MacWilliam was being hotly contested. The previous December O'Donnell had announced his intention of reviving the proscribed title and called the clans to the ancient site of Rousakeera, where Tibbot's father had finally been elected. All the septs of the Bourke clans made their way to the site only to find that most of them were barred by O'Donnell's men from attending the ceremony. O'Donnell then imposed his own choice on them, Theobald Bourke of Tirawley, a very minor player, which so enraged the rest of the Bourkes that they withdrew from any further co-operation, but before they could get away O'Donnell took several hostages, including Tibbot. However, Tibbot soon managed to escape and was now free and more than willing to enter into negotiations with Clifford.

Finally rid of Bingham, Grace wasted little time and once again turned to raiding and looting along the west coast, although in this instance it was more for basics such as food and cattle than for plunder. The Earl of Thomond reported his men having to fight off her raiders, while the Dean of Limerick noted that 'Grany ny Maly and MacNeill of Barra in Scotland' had recently raided each other's property. The Dean did not say who had struck first but, given her past history, one would bet on Grace.

Clifford's attitude and methods were totally different from those of Bingham. He already had a link with Tibbot through Tibbot's brother-in-law, Donough O'Connor of Sligo, who was resident at the English Court where the two men had met and become friends. Clifford retook Sligo Castle from O'Donnell and installed

Donough on the understanding that he should set about establishing 'friendship and concord' between himself and Tibbot and the young Richard Bourke (the Devil's Hook's son), and they, and a handful of minor chiefs, made a formal agreement with Clifford and were pardoned – again – for all 'past offences'. But this time, rather than fining Tibbot and the rest, Clifford provided them with cattle to enable them to restock their herds, in return for their promising to repay the arrears of their Composition rents and support the Governor thereafter.

For Tibbot nothing could have been better. Reinforced now by Clifford's own troops, he marched into Tirawley and 'banished' the MacWilliam whom O'Donnell had forced on the Bourkes. He then went to Clifford with a list of fourteen demands in exchange for his service, demands which he wished to be put before the Privy Council. Most of them were agreed, including the one that he should be given a title. He was granted the lands of those within his own clan who had been killed in the previous rebellion and in future would receive a company of foot soldiers to be paid for by the English government. He also secured pensions for several members of his family, including his uncle, Donal of the Pipes. Grace, too, was not forgotten. The Lord Deputy himself gave Tibbot 'and his mother' £200 for services at sea. But as we shall see, Tibbot was still playing a deep game of his own.

The Bourkes could not remain unscathed by the Ulster war for long. In August 1598, after the English were well and truly beaten at the Battle of Yellow Ford, O'Donnell again moved on Mayo, raiding and plundering at will. Enraged at what he saw as Tibbot's defection to the enemy, he paid particular attention to Grace's own lands around Burrishoole and Murrisk, and yet again they were laid waste, though she herself seems to have been safe enough in her castle at Rockfleet.

There is a reference to Grace in 1601 in a report from a Captain Plessington of the English warship, the *Tremontana*, which was cruising up and down the coast of Donegal charged with intercepting any ships from Spain coming in with supplies for the rebels following reports that two Spanish vessels, bearing 'treasure' and munitions, had over the previous Christmas put first into Clew Bay then into Teelin and Killybegs to unload. While on patrol he met up with a galley of 'thirty eight oars with one hundred shot on board', which he forced to run on to the rocks between Teelin and Killybeg. The men on the galley fired on the *Tremontana*, which then settled the matter with her guns. Plessington reported that 'this galley came out of Connaught and belongs to Grany O'Malley whose base son was her captain'. It almost certainly was one of Grace's ships, though she was not on board, but he was wrong about her captain, for Grace had no 'base son'. The captain was unlikely to have been Murrough, and was possibly Tibbot, but it is suggested that it is more likely to have been another relative and that the error must have arisen in 'the interpretation of information given in Irish'.

This is the very last contemporary mention of Grace. The rest is silence. Most remarkably, she simply disappears without trace. There is not even a record of when or where she died. Dates are variously given as 1600 or 1603 and the place as either Rockfleet or Clare Island, where some legends have it that she spent her last years 'in an abbey', though this might simply mean that she is buried in the Cistercian abbey ruins.

The fact remains that we simply do not know what happened to Grace. That snapper-up of unconsidered trifles, H.V. Morton, tells two strange tales. One is that 'for many years on Clare Island her skull was decorated with ribbons and shown to visitors', which is firmly denied in Mayo. Another, truly scurrilous, is that in the nineteenth century a company was formed in Scotland for the acquisition of bones for use on the land as fertiliser. A ship raided the west coast of Ireland, having learned there were quantities of bones to be had 'piled up in churchyards and old abbeys', and Grace's bones 'went to manure a Scottish acre'. However, Grace, from wherever she was, set out to punish such desecration and 'one of her grinders, discovered in a turnip, choked to death the Scotsman who ate it'.

In the *Choreographical Description of West Connaught*, written in 1684 as a description of the country, rather than as a history, R.A. O'Flaherty says that she (Grace) 'is now most vividly remembered by tradition. People were living in the last generation who conversed with her, people who knew her personally. Charles Cormick of Erris, now seventy-four years and six weeks old saw and conversed with Elizabeth O'Donnell in Newtown, who died about sixty-four years ago, who remembered Grainne-na-Cearbach, [as did] also a Mr Walsh, who died at the age of 107 who claimed to have been a foster brother of hers' and that she was the 'most celebrated personage of her family that ever lived, Grace of the Gamesters'.

15

Endgame –
The Flight of the Wild Geese

The story does not quite end here. Although Grace disappears from history, during the last years of her life she must have been aware of, possibly even encouraged, the underhand dealings of Tibbot following the defeat of the English in 1598 at the Battle of Yellow Ford. In spite of virtually all his demands being met and the allegiance he freely offered to Clifford and, through him, to the Crown, his loyalties proved to be as shifting and complex as those of his mother. His one abiding loyalty after the death of his step-brother Edmund was to his O'Flaherty half-brother, Murrough. It might be assumed that, having achieved more or less all that he wanted, from then on he would finally keep his promises, not least because Clifford was a fair man with whom he apparently got on; except that for a few heady months following the Battle of Yellow Ford it looked as if a miracle might happen and the English be driven out.

The defeat at Yellow Ford with the loss of over 12,000 men was one of a devastating series of blows suffered by Elizabeth during that year. Not the least of these was the death of the aged William Cecil, the Lord of Burleigh, her oldest and truest adviser. He had continued to work for her until the very end of his life, and when he was dying she sat for hours at his bedside, feeding him with her own hands. On his death, writes A.L. Rowse, 'she wept for the years that were over; for herself and the few years that remained without him: the years that were to bring her greatest grief in the death of Essex, who should have been her son, whose stepfather was Leicester', a reference to Robert Dudley, Earl of Leicester, the one man she really did love. After Burleigh's death she finally conferred on his son Robert, that spinner of webs of intrigue, the position of Secretary of State to the Privy Council (and with it that of spymaster), thus paving the way for him to develop even further his contacts with Edinburgh.

At least Grace did outlive her greatest enemy, for in the aftermath of Yellow Ford, when experience of those who fought in Ireland was at a premium, Sir Richard Bingham was released from the Fleet, reinstated and sent over to Ireland, the Queen informing whoever it might concern that he was returning 'with our favour and gracious opinion'. But his triumph was short-lived. After being involved in a single attack outside Dublin, he died, apparently of natural causes.

Following Yellow Ford, O'Neill was now triumphant throughout the north of Ireland, holding Ulster himself, while Hugh O'Donnell was in almost complete control of Connaught, promptly returning his own 'MacWilliam' to Mayo. It was this ancient, vexed title that above all else kept Tibbot at least nominally on the side of the Crown even though he must have recognised there was no future in what has been well described as 'a doomed title in a doomed world'; hence his desire to acquire an English one. However, it was no longer the title he coveted, but the lands that went with it.

After Ulster and Connaught, the victors turned their attention to Munster, sweeping into the province in force. Even given that atrocity stories grow in the telling, there are sufficient grounds to believe that at least some of the reports from those on the ground are true. Refugees from the fighting were found on the road with their tongues cut out, and the Chief Justice of Munster, Chief Justice Saxey, reports that 'infants [were] taken from the nurse's breast and their brains dashed against the walls, the heart plucked out of the body in view of the wife who was forced to yield the use of her apron to wipe the blood off from the murderer's fingers...' Castles fell to the raiders, towns were burned. Both Edmund Spenser and Sir Walter Raleigh barely escaped with their lives, and it was said that Spenser lost a son in the burning of his castle, but this is no longer thought to be the case. In 1599 Clifford, who had done so much to reconcile Connaught, was killed in what became known as the Battle of Curlew Mountain. As for Tibbot, an intelligence report of that year states that he was in secret negotiation with both Hugh O'Donnell in Connaught and 'Tyrone' (O'Neill) in Ulster and that the latter and Tibbot were 'agreed but they will not have any know of it'.

Desperate measures were needed. Throughout the autumn of 1598 there was a major levy of men throughout the country and seasoned soldiers were recalled from the Low Countries. The preferred commander for the English in Ireland was Charles Blount, Lord Mountjoy, an experienced soldier and administrator. But Essex objected and pleaded with the Queen that she should give the post to him, in spite of his recent and costly fiasco off the Azores when he missed intercepting a Spanish Plate Fleet. Unfortunately, as was so often the case when it came to Essex, Elizabeth's emotions overruled her head: she gave him command of the English army in Ireland. Already ennobled as Earl Marshal of England, he did not consider the title of Lord Deputy good enough for him and demanded that of 'Lord Lieutenant', in effect Viceroy, the first person to be so designated since the Earl of Sussex over fifty years earlier. Finally, after an extraordinary series of exhibitions of arrogance, during which he set up the backs of half the Court, in March 1599 he left for Ireland, riding through a 'double lane of cheering citizens four miles long'.

After which came anti-climax as months passed during which Essex did virtually nothing (while running up enormous costs), in spite of being urged into action not only by the Privy Council but in personal letters from Elizabeth herself while O'Neill did as he pleased. Tibbot, meanwhile, who had been leading an army in the Queen's pay on what has been described as a 'dubious' term of duty in Munster, had returned to Mayo to discover that the unelected MacWilliam was back again and decided to settle the matter on his own terms. He convened a meeting of the Bourkes at the ancient site of Roskeena, where his own father had been elected to the title, and in spite of the rival claim conferred it on Grace's grandson, his old ally Richard Bourke, son of the Devil's Hook.

For a brief while the country was in a state of uneasy truce, during which Essex embarked on a series of actions which amounted almost to suicidal folly, entering into secret talks with O'Neill (who could run rings round him), firstly with a view to getting himself off the hook without having to fight, but more to the point, with an eye to what the future might hold following the death of the Queen. After all, the event could not be that far off and it was as well to plan ahead. Feeling very pleased with himself, he then bragged about his cleverness to one of his own favourites who, in turn, passed this interesting information on to his own male lover. Unsurprisingly, intelligence of what was afoot rapidly got out. As soon as he realised what had happened, Essex set off on his famous mad race to London, bursting in on the Queen before she was even dressed in order to get in his own version of events first. Yet again she forgave him, but within a year he had died on the scaffold, executed for treason following his own abortive rebellion.

His place in Ireland was finally given to Lord Mountjoy who took up the post in January 1600 at the age of thirty-six. He had given a great deal of time and thought to the situation facing him and almost immediately set up a series of garrisons strategically placed to prevent groups of rebels being able to aid each other. He also brought with him tried and trusted subordinates, installing Sir George Carew as President of Munster. Interestingly, he was also prepared to employ galloglas, and there is a story that he had his horse shot from under him while his personal galloglas was standing beside him, holding his helmet, and that the next shot hit the helmet but spared both Mountjoy and the galloglas. But the redshanks and the galloglas had suffered heavy losses during the last decade of fighting and the Battle of Kinsale, followed by the accession of James VI to the English throne, would see the end of their involvement in the Irish wars and of a custom that had lasted for centuries. However, those who had settled, mainly in County Antrim, settled in Ireland for good.

Tibbot was now receiving overtures from both sides, secretly declaring his support for each and managing to get by without openly making a decision. Then on 23 September 1601 the help promised O'Neill by Spain finally arrived in the form of 3,184 men led by Don Juan de Aguila, an experienced commander. But once again the weather played the Spaniards false, scattering the troopships and forcing them to land the soldiers at Kinsale, about as far as possible from where they were needed, with the result that O'Donnell and O'Neill had to race south with all the dangers that posed.

This suited Mountjoy, carefully planning his moves and his battle plan, determined that there would be no re-run of Yellow Ford. For two months there was a virtual stand-off. At the beginning of December Tibbot marched south from Mayo at the head of three hundred men to join the battle, neither Mountjoy nor O'Neill knowing which side he intended to support. At the last moment Tibbot sided with Mountjoy. Fortunately for him, the English won. According to Knox, after 1601 there was no more fighting in Mayo, and at the end of the Nine Years War in 1607 O'Donnell and his MacWilliam went with O'Neill and the rest of the Irish nobility, known as 'the Wild Geese', into permanent exile in Spain. 'The name of "MacWilliam" disappeared,' he writes, 'and the Gaelic tribal organisation disappeared with that great name forever.'

If Grace was still alive in March 1603, then she also outlasted Elizabeth, living to see a Scots King on the English throne. Not long after King James's accession 'Tibbot-ne-Long', now by far the biggest landowner in Mayo, was knighted for his 'loyal and valorous service', taking the name Sir Tibbot Bourke. King James also formally appointed Mountjoy Lord Lieutenant of Ireland and created him Earl of Devonshire. In 1627, a year after the death of his half-brother Murrough, Tibbot acquired another title, that of Viscount Mayo, this time at the hands of King Charles I. This is particularly remarkable, as to the end of his days he was never trusted by the English, and rightly so. He would never change and up until his own demise, at Kinturk Castle in 1629, he was scheming and plotting with the very exiles in Spain against whom he had fought at Kinsale. Like mother, like son.

My search for Grace grew out of a continuing interest in those women, often relatively unknown and of whom there are a number of examples, who made lives for themselves well outside the bounds of what was considered acceptable in the era into which they were born. Grace's story turned out to be a strange and complex one. On the face of it, it is one of high romance and that is certainly the angle which is promoted in Ireland today. Like her later counterparts, Mary Read and Anne Bonnie, she strides her deck, brave, beautiful, gallant in love and war. But it is a great deal more complicated than that.

Closer study shows two very definite sides to Grace. The obvious divide is between Grace as a 'real' person and how she is portrayed in myth and legend, but again it is not that simple. From what we know of the first part of her life, up to her second marriage, much of it is indeed the stuff of storybooks. It is that of the child who cut off her hair so that her father would take her to sea, the young wife who more or less took over her husband's role in his clan and then turned to piracy, the woman who rescued a shipwrecked stranger, fell in love with him, and after his brutal murder avenged his death. Even then, though, it is necessary to look, as it were, behind the film script.

She was not called 'the Pirate Queen' for nothing. To hold that title she had to be as ruthless and tough as any man. She led her men not only in the battles that ensued when they boarded a ship but also on land, when the fancy took her. She was prepared to kill and be killed in the days when fighting was hand-to-hand. Little wonder, then, that when off duty she drank, gambled, swore and slept around. So she is hardly the heroine of conventional romance.

But there is an even bigger gulf between the Grace of those early days and the later one. When she was born, English influence, as we have seen, was pretty minimal outside the Pale and almost entirely absent in Mayo; the old Gaelic laws and customs still applied. Life, therefore, went on much as it had for centuries, thus enabling her to establish her system of piracy on the west coast. However, even given that what she spent much of her time doing was against the law, there is no record of her becoming directly involved in the continuous inter-clan warfare until forced to do so, first on the death of her husband when the Joyces retook Hen Castle, then to avenge the death of her lover, nor is there any record of her being thought of as particularly devious.

But from the accession of Elizabeth in 1558 there came a seachange, gradual at first, then gathering momentum, until English influence and virtual colonial rule spread across the whole of Ireland, assisted by the planting of settlers and enforced by armies. So now, as well as inter-clan rivalry and family feuds, there was the ongoing enemy, the invader from across the Irish Sea. From the 1560s onwards there was no stability, hardly any period without substantial bloodshed. From an English view-point, possibly the closest analogy is that of the period following the Norman invasion, although that did not, thankfully, lead to a further five hundred years of conflict.

In passing, one of the real surprises that came out of researching this story was the integral, in some cases crucial, role played by the Scots in the story of sixteenth-century Ireland: the galloglas and redshanks, the profes-sional fighters described in many English histories simply as 'mercenaries', although the place of the gallo-glas in particular was somewhat different. Their pres-ence really worried the English administration and, as we have seen, what was considered to be one of Grace's greatest misdeeds was that she 'drew in the Scots'. There is scarcely a skirmish fought on Irish soil during the sixteenth century, let alone a battle, in which they did not take part.

So to the second half of Grace's life, the Grace whose life was lived out against a background of constant revolt, warfare and the relentless encroachment of English rule which was to destroy entirely her old way of life. From then on it was every man (or woman) for himself. It might well be useful to be able to handle a weapon and fight, but from her marriage to Richard Bourke, entered upon in no small part for pragmatic reasons, Grace realised that from now on she would need to use very different weapons if she and her family were to survive. Therefore, to ensure they did so, she was prepared to lie, cheat, prevaricate, fling herself when necessary on the mercy of the English government, apparently submit and go over to the enemy, then return to base and help foment revolt, taking part in anti-English rebellions, be pardoned (twice), talk to Queen Elizabeth face to face, yet turn on her own son for siding with the English, raiding his lands and killing his followers. She was even prepared to stand by while Tibbot assisted in the slaughter of over a hundred Bourkes and their followers in order to prove his loyalty to the enemy, a 'loyalty' that could be set aside at any time it suited either of them.

When it was first suggested to me that Grace might at some time have acted as an intelligencer for the English, the idea seemed far-fetched. Not any more, given her subsequent career. It seems all of a piece if it allowed her to continue unimpeded, with her policy of 'maintenance' along the west coast of Ireland, and might well have saved her twice from prison and once from certain death.

It becomes easier, therefore, to understand the reluctance of early historians to chronicle her activities. They may indeed have been biased against a woman taking on such an unsuitable role in the scheme of things, but a more believable explanation is that throughout the second half of her life she simply could not be trusted by *anyone*, anyone at all.

It would be so much easier if she could be cast in the simple role of an Irish patriot (which some would like to do), but that is impossible. At the end of the day what we have is a portrait of a woman who, in spite of everything, was independent, highly skilled, very brave and, above all, a great survivor. The reality may be harder to accept than the romance, but it is far more interesting.

Appendix One

QUEEN ELIZABETH'S REPRESENTATIVES IN IRELAND

Thomas Radcliffe, Earl of Sussex, Lord
Deputy 1559, Lord Lieutenant 1560

LORD DEPUTIES

Sir Henry Sidney	1566
Sir William Fitzwilliam	1571
Sir Henry Sidney	1575
Lord Arthur Grey de Wilton	1580
Sir John Perrott	1584
Sir William Fitzwilliam	1588
Sir William Russell	1594
Lord Thomas Burgh	1597

LORDS LIEUTENANT

Robert Devereux, Earl of Essex	1599
Charles Blount, Lord Mountjoy (first Lord Deputy, then Lord Lieutenant)	1600

Appendix Two

THE EIGHTEEN ARTICLES OF INTERROGATION AND THE RESPONSES

'TO BE ANSWERED BY GRANY NIMALY'

1. Who was her father and mother?
2. Who was her first husband?
3. What sons she had by him. What be their names and where they live?
4. What countries they have to maintain them withal?
5. To whom they be married?
6. What kin was O'Flaherty her first husband to Sirr Mourrough M'Ne Dough O'Flaherty that is here now at the Court?
7. To answer the like question for her 2 husband and for his sons and their livings.
8. If she were to be allowed her dower or thirds of her husbands living of what value the same might be of?
9. Where upon the Composition of Connaught there hath been any provision for the wives?
10. Whether it be not against the Customs of Ireland for the wives to have more after the deaths of their husbands than they brought with them.
11. How shall she hath had maintenance and living since her last husband's death?
12. Of what kindred is Walter Bourgh fitz Tibalds and Shane Bourk mcMoyler to her son?
13. What captains and countries lie next her first husband's possessions?
14. Who doth possess the house of Moriske upon the seaside in Owle O'Maly?
15. What lands doth McGibbon possess in that country?
16. Who doth possess the country named Carramore and Mayn Connell?

17. Who doth possess the island of Achill and Kill Castle?
18. What kin was her last husband to Walter and Ulick Bourke?

ANSWERS OF GRANY NIMALY TO THE ARTICLES

To the First

Her father was called Doodarro O'Mailly sometime chieftain of the country called Opper Owle O'Mailly now called the barony of Murasky (Moriske) her mother was called Margaret my Mailly daughter to Conogher Omailly of the said country and family. The whole country of Owle O Mailly aforesaid have these islands viz. Inish Boffyn Cleria Inish Twirke Inish arke Caher Inishdalluff Davellen and other small islands of little value and the rest of the mainland are divided into towns to the number of twenty, and to every town four quarters or ploughs of land, is assigned; out of every such quarter of land is yearly paid to her Majesty ten shillings, called the composition rent. There is also in Connaught a country called Owle Eighter, otherwise the Lower or Nether Owle, containing fifty towns at four quarters the town, yearly paying the same rent, whereof the Sept of the Mailles in general hath twenty towns, the Bourkes of MacWilliam country other twenty towns and the Earl of Ormond ten towns.

To the Second

Her first husband was called Donell Ichoggy O'Flaherty and during his life chieftain of the Barony of Bally-ne-henssy, containing twenty four towns at four quarters of land to every town paying yearly the Composition rent aforesaid. After his death Teige O'Flaherty the eldest son of Sir Mourrough now at court entered into Bally-ne-hennsy aforesaid ther and did build a strong castle and the same with the demesne lands thereof kept many years. Which Teige in the last rebellion of his father was slain.

To the Third

She had two sons by her said first husband the eldest called Owen O'Flaherty married Katherine Bourke daughter of Edmond Bourke of Castle Barry by her he had a son named Donell O'Flaherty, now living which Owen all his lifetime remained a true subject to Her Majestie under the government of Sir Nicholas Malby while he lived and under Sir Richard Bingham until July 1586 at which time the Bourkes of the McWilliams country and the sept of the Shoose began to rebel. The said Owen according to Sir Richard's special direction, did withdraw himself his followers and tenants, with all their goods and cattle into a strong island for their more and better assurance. Then having been set against the said rebels five hundred soldiers under the leading of Capt John Bingham appointed by his brother Richard Bingham as the lieutenant in those parts. When they missed both the rebels and the cattle they came to the mainland right against the said island calling for victualls whereupon the said Owen came forth with a number of boats and ferried all the soldiers into the island where they were entertained with the best cheer they had. That night the said Owen was apprehended and tied with a rope with eighteen of his chief followers; in the morning the soldiers drew out of the island four thousand cows, five hundred stud mares and horses and a thousand sheep leaving the remainder of the poor men all naked within the island . . . came with the cattle and prisoners to Bally-ne-henssy aforsaid where John Bingham aforsaid stayed for their coming; that evening he caused the said eighteen persons without trial or good cause to be hanged among whom was hanged a gentleman of land and living called Thebault O'Twohill being of the age of four score and ten years. The next night following a false alarm was raised in the camp in the dead of night the said Owen being fast bound in the cabin

[184]

of Captain Grene O'Mulloy and at that instant the said Owen was cruelly murdered having 12 deadly wounds and in that miserable sort he ended his years and unfortunate days. Captain William Mostyn now at court and Captain Meriman and Captain Mordant were of that company. Her second son called Morrough O'Flaherty, now living, is married to Honora Bourke daughter of Richard Bourke of Deriviclaghny in the Magtheri Reagh within the county of Galway.

To the Fourth
Morrough her second son aforsaid and Donell son to her first son, the aforsaid Owen murdered, do possess and enjoy the fourth part of the Barony of Bally-ne-henssy aforsaid until them descended from their ancestors which is all the maintenance they have.

To the Fifth
This is answered more at larger in the answer to the third article.

To the Sixth
Her first husband the mother side's of Sir Morrough now at court was her cousins germain and also cousins, both being descended of one stock and root, of nine degrees of consanguinity asunder.

To the Seventh
Her second husband was called Sir Richard Bourke Knight alias McWilliam chief of the Bourkes of Nether or Low Connaught by him she had a son called Theobald Bourke now living he is married to Maeve O'Connor sister to O'Connor Sligo now at court, his inheritance is about 40 quarters of land situated in the three baronies of Carry, Nether Owle and Galling.

To the Eighth
The countries of Connaught among the Irishry never yielded any thirds to any woman surviving the chieftain whose rent was uncertain for the most part extorted but now made certain by the Composition and all Irish exactions merely abolished.

To the Ninth
The Composition provided nothing to relieve the wife of any chieftain after his death, wherein no mention is made of any such.

To the Tenth
Among the Irishry the custom is that wives shall have but her first dowry without any increase or allowance for the same, time out of mind it hath been so used, and before any woman do deliver up her marriage portion to her husband she receives sureties for the restitution of the same in manner and form as she hath delivered it, in regard that husband through their great expenses especially chieftains at the time of their deaths have no goods to leave behind them but are commonly indebted; at other times they are divorced upon proof of precontracts; and the husband now and then without any lawful or due proceedings 'do put his wife from him' and so bringeth in another; so as the wife is to have sureties for her dowry for fear of the worse.

To the Eleventh
After the death of her last husband she gathered together all her own followers and with 1000 head of cows and mares departed and became a dweller in Caarrikhowly in Borisoole parcel of the Earl of Ormond's lands in Connaught and in the year 1586 after the murdering of her son Owen the rebellion being then in Connaught, Sir Richard Bingham granted her his letters of tuition against

all men and will her to remove from her late dwelling at Borrisoole and to come and dwell under him, in her journey as she travelled was encountered by five bands of soldiers under the leading of John Bingham and thereupon she was apprehended and tied in a rope, both she and her followers at that instant were spoiled of their said cattle and of all that ever they had besides the same and brought to Sir Richard who caused a new pair of gallows to be made for her last funeral where she thought to end her life, she was let at liberty upon the hostage and pledge of one Richard Bourke otherwise called the Devil's Hook when he did rebel, fear compelled her to fly by sea into Ulster and there with O'Neill and O'Donnell stayed three months; her galleys by a tempest being broken. She returned to Connaught and in Dublin received her Majestie's pardon by Sir John Perrot six years past and so made free. Ever since she dwelleth in Connaught a farmers life very poor bearing cess and paying Her Majesty's Composition rent, utterly did she give over her former trade of maintenance by sea and land.

To the Twelfth
Walter Bourke FitzThebalt and Shane Bourke FitzMeller are cousins german removed of one side viz. Walter son to Thebault, son to Meiller of the said Walter Foady. Thebault Bourke mentioned in the seventh article and born by Grace by Mailly son to Sir Richard Bourke her last husband, which Sir Richard was brother to the said Walter Foady.

To the Thirteenth
The country of her first husband is situated between Owle O'Mailley on the north west part, Mac William's country to the north east towards the country of Sligo, Sir Morrough O'Flahertys country; and on the east side towards Galway and the great bay of Galway on the south.

To the Fourteenth

The castle town and lands of Morisky is possessed by Owen McThomas O'Mailley, now chietain by the name of O'Mailley.

To the Fifteenth

The Mac Gibbons have no lands by inheritence in any part of the country; farmers they are at will both to the Bourkes and to the O'Maillies.

To the Sixteenth

She doth not know or understand Caremore or Moinconnell.

To the Seventeenth

The Island of Ackhill is occupied by some of the Mailleys as tenants to the Earl of Ormond, as for Kill castle, she knoweth no town of that name.

To the Eighteenth

Her last husband had two brothers Walter and Ulick Bourke both died before she married Sir Richard Bourke, her said husband, their father was called David Bourke.

Author's note. The above is taken from the relevant volume of the Calendars of State Papers (Domestic), edited by Hans Claude Hamilton (1890), Vol. CLXX, pp. 132/133, in the Bodleian Library, Oxford.

Bibliography

PRIMARY SOURCE MATERIAL

State Papers of Ireland, Public Record Office, London. Under general shelf mark 63. Volumes: 19, 74, 145, 146, 147, 158, 170, 171, 172, 179 (all indexed).

Calendars of State Papers (Domestic), Bodleian Library, Oxford. Ed. Hans Claude Hamilton., F.S.A. 1508–73, 1574–85, 1588–92, 1592–96, 1599–1600. Volumes XLI, LXXXIV, XVI, LXI, CCVI, CCVII, CCVIII, CXL VI, CLI, CLXX, CLXXI, CLXXII, CLXVI, CXXII, XCIX (all indexed).

Calendars of Carew Manuscripts, Trinity College, Dublin. Ed. Brewer and Bullen, London 1869. Edition 1974.

Calendar of the Manuscripts of the Most. Hon, Marquis of Salisbury, KG. Volume IV. London 1883.

EARLY SOURCES

T. Derricke. *Images of Ireland 1581*, ed. J. Small. Belfast 1985.

A Choreographical Description of the Territory of West or H-Iar Connaught AD 1684 by Roderick O'Flaherty. From Mss in Trinity College, Dublin, with notes by James Hardiman MRIA. Dublin 1846.

Letters Containing Information Relative to the County of Mayo – Ordnance Survey Volumes 1 and 2 1838. Transcribed by M.O. Flanagan 1927. Typescript in British Library.

J. Perrot. *The Chronicles of Ireland 1584–1608*, ed. H. Wood. Dublin 1933.

SECONDARY SOURCES

Bagwell, R. *Ireland Under the Tudors*. London 1885–90.

Chambers, Anne. *Granuaile*. Dublin 1974 and 1998.

Curtis, E. *A History of Ireland*. London 1936.

Doyle, Henry. *Illustrated History of Ireland*. Dublin 1868.

Ellis, S.G. *Ireland Under the Tudors*. London 1985.

— *Ireland in the Age of the Tudors*. London 1998.

Falls, Cyril. *Elizabeth's Irish Wars*. London 1950.

Graham, W. *The Spanish Armadas*. London 1972.

Jenkins, E. *Elizabeth the Great*. London 1958.

Knox, H. *The History of the County of Mayo*. London 1908.

Lennon, C. *Sixteenth Century Ireland – The Incomplete Conquest*. Dublin 1994.

Macdonald, T. *Achill Island*. Dublin 1997.

Magnusson, M. *Landlord and Tenant: A View of Irish History*. London 1978.

Marsden, J. *Galloglas: Hebridean and West Highland Mercenary Warrior Kindreds in Medieval Ireland*. East Linton 2003.

Maxwell, C. *The Stranger in Ireland*. Dublin 1954.

Morton, G. *Elizabethan Ireland*. London 1971.

Morton, H.V. *In Search of Ireland*. London 1930.

Otway, C. *A Tour of Connaught*. Dublin 1839.

Oxford History of Ireland, ed. R.F. Foster. Oxford 1992.

Prebble, J. *The Lion in the North*. London. 1983 edition.

Rowse, A.L. *The England of Elizabeth*. London 1950.

— *Queen Elizabeth and Her Subjects* (with G.B. Harrison). London 1935.

Sidney, Sir Henry. *Irish Narratives*, ed. Ciaran Brady. Cork 2002.

Young, J. *Social History of 16th Century Britain*. London 1984.

Index